109 Walks

IN BRITISH COLUMBIA'S LOWER MAINLAND

Second Edition

By Mary and David Macaree

Douglas & McIntyre
Vancouver/Toronto

The Mountaineers
Seattle

Published in the United States by The Mountaineers
306 2nd Ave. West, Seattle, WA 98119

The Mountaineers: Organized 1906 "to explore, study, preserve and
enjoy the natural beauty of the Northwest."

Library of Congress Cataloguing in Publication Data

Macaree, Mary.
    109 walks in British Columbia's lower mainland

    Rev. ed. of: 109 walks in B. C.'s lower mainland. 1976.
    Bibliography: p.
    1. Hiking – British Columbia – Guide-books. 2. Trails –
British Columbia – Guide-books. 3. Natural history –
British Columbia. 4. British Columbia – Description and
travel – Guide-books. I. Macaree, David, II. Title.
III. Title. One hundred nine walks in British Columbia's
lower mainland. IV. Title: One hundred and nine walks
in British Columbia's lower mainland.
    GV199.44.C22B747 1983   917.11'044   82-22496
    ISBN 0-89886-068-7 (pbk.)

Published in Canada by Douglas & McIntyre Ltd.
1615 Venables Street, Vancouver, BC V5L 2H1

Canadian Cataloguing in Publication Data

Macaree, Mary.
    109 walks in British Columbia's Lower
Mainland

    Rev. ed of: 109 walks in B. C.'s lower mainland. 1976.
    Bibliography p.
    Includes index.
    ISBN 0-88894-380-6

    1. Walking – British Columbia – Lower
Mainland Region – Guide-books. 2. Trails –
British Columbia – Lower Mainland Region –
Guide-books. 3. Lower Mainland Region (B. C.)
– Description and travel – Guide-books. I.
Macaree, David. II. Title.
    GV199.44.C22B74 1983   917.11'33044
                                C83-091035-2

Cover photograph: Fraser Valley from Sumas Peak, by Mary Macaree
Maps by Mary Macaree
Printed and bound in Canada

CONTENTS

Siwash Rock from Merilees Trail

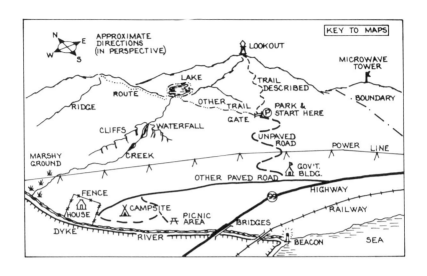

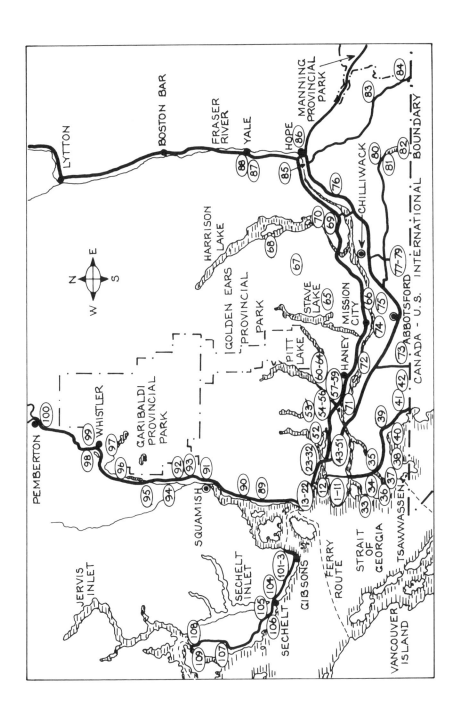

7

Columnar basalt (Walk 95)

INTRODUCTION

Public acceptance of this work's first edition has made necessary the pleasant task of preparing a second. As before, we have tried to ensure that no walk is more than an easy day's excursion, generally four hours or less for the total trip. The trips, too, tend to be at a low level, with significant gain in height limited to a relatively few instances.

The main function of **109 Walks** is, quite simply, utilitarian, the descriptions representing as accurately as possible the state of trails and the means of vehicle approach at the time of printing; we cannot, of course, accept responsibility for changes that may occur subsequently. Despite the emphasis on usefulness, however, we hope that readers will obtain aesthetic pleasure in browsing through the text with its accompanying maps and photographs so that the total effect is enjoyable as well as instructive.

Naturally our book focusses mainly on the lower mainland's population centres: Vancouver and the municipalities bordering on the city. We assume, though, that many readers will want to combine drives into the country with walks close to their destinations whereas others will be happy to have outings described in the vicinity of campgrounds where they may be staying for a day or so.

The arrangement of contents, therefore, consists of the city itself, the north shore of Burrard Inlet, then districts south of the metropolitan area—mainly Delta, Richmond, and Surrey—followed by areas to the east as far as Pitt River. Next come accounts of walks close to the main radiating routes: Highway 7 (the Lougheed) along the north side of the Fraser Valley, and Highway 1 south of the river as far as Hope and a little beyond, these being followed by Highway 99 to Squamish and Pemberton, with a foray across Howe Sound to the Sechelt Peninsula. In addition to the detailed descriptions, we give brief synopses of fifty-one other walks in an appendix for those who wish short outings or like poking about in out-of-the-way places.

A compilation such as this does not claim to be exhaustive; in the nature of things it provides only a sampling—an attractive one, we hope. One sad feature, though, is the forced omission of certain walks because their approaches have been blocked off by the activities of developers, both public and private, accompanied by dissuasive "No Trespassing" signs. Controversy over the Ross Dam on the Skagit River makes doubtful one or two walks at the south end of that valley as well. It is easy to become emotional about such matters; it must be conceded, though, that indifference has been a contributory factor and, what is worse, so has user misbehaviour—ranging from simple carelessness and failure to respect privacy to deliberate acts of vandalism. The only way to offset the latter is through education in good trail manners, and in this respect parents may play a major role by impressing on youngsters this simple rule: LEAVE ONLY FOOTPRINTS; TAKE ONLY PHOTOGRAPHS.

Frost crystals

It is particularly distressing to find instances of wilful damage in parks and recreation areas that have already been secured for public use, because here the vandal is destroying the property of all his fellow citizens. Not all of this can be attributed to walkers, of course; the trail bike is one of the most destructive agents of the recreational environment. The presence of these machines and their thoughtless riders is not only offensive because of the pollution they create with their noise and stench; the effects of their activity remain after them in the form of damage to trails, carved into deep ruts, and to plants, broken and twisted. When, in addition, it is considered that they waste nonrenewable natural resources, it is difficult to understand why their users receive government encouragement, and why parents are so foolish as to supply youngsters with such dangerous toys.

A more cheerful note is the recent change in attitude of the forest companies towards multiple use of woodlands, resulting in the opening up of new areas to public access when logging is not going on. To encourage this more liberal policy, it should hardly be necessary to stress the need to respect the companies' property and to obey signs. Admittedly, routes through recently logged sections do not make for the most attractive walking; moves are now afoot, however, to retain treed corridors in scenic locations, and the availability of logging roads, even if only on weekends, does give access to new country. At that, lumbering operations are less messy than some ski areas in summer, the debris and scalped slopes sometimes being little better than ecological disasters.

The most encouraging feature, however, is the increasing involvement of various levels of government in the establishment of parks and recreational corridors. One agency instrumental in putting people back on their feet is the Parks and Outdoor Recreation Division. The activity of this body has created good trails in a number of areas: Alice Lake and Golden Ears, to name only two. The single criticism—a surprising one, perhaps—is that some of them are too good with their easy grades and long zigzags, leading to corner cutting and consequent damage. In addition, the B.C. Ministry of Forests has developed wilderness recreation sites, often in areas where logging is going on, and has marked various trails. In rural areas, too, regional districts have assumed direct responsibility for some recreation sites, Campbell Valley and Aldergrove being specially noteworthy.

Nor should the initiative of various outdoor clubs go unrecorded since these were, in many instances, the original creators of trails into scenic areas. Member groups of the Federation of Mountain Clubs of British Columbia have assumed responsibility for certain trails and carry on periodic trail-clearing bees. In this context, too, the Centennial Trail created by the Canadian Hostelling Association should be mentioned, several of the walks described herein being along stretches of that route to the interior. Similarly, reference may be made to the Baden-Powell Trail along the North Shore, even though some parts of it have fallen on evil days because of hostility by various individuals.

Glacial scoring, record of the rocks

All in all, though, the picture is brighter than it was a few years ago. More people are walking and more attention is being given to requests for access to the countryside. It is our hope that this book will serve as an added stimulus to set more people's feet on the paths of this part of British Columbia. If we achieve this aim, our thanks must go to a number of individuals, private citizens and representatives of official bodies alike. Members of the GVRD Parks and Outdoor Recreation Division were particularly helpful in responding to our requests for information, but so also were those of the Fish and Wildlife Branch, and the Ministry of Forests.

In fact, information is available from a variety of sources, public and private. The larger parks have their own centres that provide trail maps; in others, park personnel will help. All existing guides may be obtained on request from Ministry of Lands, Parks, and Housing, Parks and Outdoor Recreation Division, 1019 Wharf Street, Victoria, B.C. V8W 2Y9, and a selection of these is available in tourist information centres—for example, the office located on Highway 1 east of Abbotsford. Notes on Forest Service recreational sites, too, are procurable from local district offices of the ministry.

To build up a personal stock of maps, you may begin with those of Vancouver, the Fraser Valley, and the Sunshine Coast published by Dominion Map Limited, 571 Howe Street, Vancouver, V6C 2C2; this firm can also supply sheets of the 1:50,000 National Topographic Series as well as the recreation map of the Whistler area produced by the Outdoor Recreation Council. Topographic maps may also be obtained in Vancouver from Renouf Books at 522 West Hastings V6B 1L6, or from Geological Survey of Canada, 100 West Pender V6B 1R8.

Besides the sheer enjoyment involved in getting back the use of your limbs and escaping from your fellow human beings, your excursions outdoors should increase your awareness of nature in at least some of its manifestations: flowers and shrubs of summer, the trees of the forest and its wildlife, the record of the rocks, land features, and waterways. You will find brief comments on some of these topics in our descriptions of various walks, but these are to be considered only as appetite stimulators to send you to the appropriate authority for more information. The same applies to human activity, even to the factors involved in giving names to places, a topic exhaustively covered in the first work listed. One unfortunate lack is a good, up-to-date, general history of the area; local groups have done studies of municipalities such as Langley, Mission, and Yale, and of course Vancouver has been well covered, but no overall survey exists. Surely here is a worthwhile project for some local historian.

USEFUL BOOKS

Akrigg, G. P. V., and Akrigg, H. B. **1001 British Columbia Place Names.** 3rd ed. Vancouver: Discovery Press, 1973.

Kalman, Harold. **Exploring Vancouver: Ten Tours of the City and its Buildings.** Revised ed. Vancouver: University of B.C. Press, 1978.

Lyons, C. P. **Trees, Shrubs and Flowers to Know in British Columbia.** 3rd ed. Vancouver: Dent, 1966.

Morley, Alan. **Vancouver: From Milltown to Metropolis.** Revised 5th ed. Vancouver: Mitchell Press, 1974.

Peterson, Roger Tory. **Field Guide to Western Birds.** 2nd ed. Boston: Houghton Miffin, 1972.

Prescott, Christine, and Cavin, Betty. **A Nature Walk in Stanley Park.** Vancouver: Mitchell Press, 1977.

Robbins, C. S., et al. **Birds of North America: A Guide to Field Identification.** New York: Golden Press, 1966.

1 UBC GARDENS (North)

Round trip 3.6 km (2.2 mi)
Allow 1.5 hours
Good all year

It is unfortunate that the University of British Columbia, despite its superb setting on Point Grey, provides a minimum of inspiring architecture. For this reason, a walk on its campus is best described in terms of its various gardens where, especially in spring and summer, art and nature harmonize. In fact, you may enjoy a kind of world tour—a rose garden in the European style, a Japanese landscape in miniature, a park with totem poles and related West Coast Indian artifacts, plus a cliff-top display of perennials and heathers set against a background of sea and mountains.

A good place to begin this outing is by the bus terminal on University Boulevard, west of the swimming pool. From here, walk uphill to the Main Mall and turn right, passing the War Memorial Cairn before traversing the roof of Sedgewick Library. At its north end, go left past the south façade of the Fine Arts Building and its neighbour, Music, the latter with its symbolic metal piece, *Tuning Fork*. Next, descend the steps to pass the Armoury and cross the West Mall to pick up a path going to the right in a narrow grove of trees, passing the Asian Studies Building, a memento of Osaka's World Fair.

Now, as you bear left, you find yourself in an attractively laid out oriental garden, a foretaste of Nitobe Memorial Garden (small admission charge) with its ornamental gate and its miniscule rendering of a whole landscape: a river system from mountain stream to deltaic marshland, complete with a

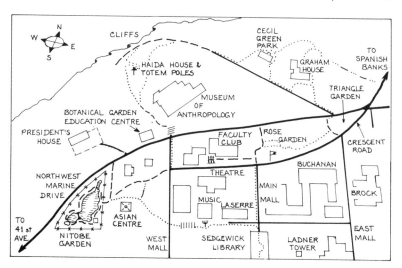

Nitobe Japanese Garden

lake stocked with large carp and surrounded by trees, which make a rare show of blossoms in spring. There is even a Japanese teahouse, expertly reconstructed.

When you re-emerge, turn left, then go right on a path among the trees south of International House. By so doing, you reach the West Mall a short distance from its junction with Marine Drive. Cross the latter thoroughfare and proceed northward by a path to the left of the Museum of Anthropology to pay your respects to the Native Indian long-house and totem poles. From here, you continue to the cliff edge with its striking views across Burrard Inlet to Howe Sound, with Mount Wrottesley framed in the background.

But you are not yet finished. Continue eastward on the track that becomes a road, actually a one-time section of Marine Drive and now a dead end. Turn left into the gardens of Cecil Green House, home of the UBC Alumni Association, then make a similar circuit of its next-door neighbour, Graham House. Now, recross Marine Drive and pass the Triangle Garden to see another highlight, the Rose Garden, reached by turning right towards the flagpole, itself the location of another inspiring viewpoint.

From here you may either return directly along the Main Mall or make a slight detour along the front of the Faculty Club to examine at close quarters the fountain by the Graduate Student Centre and its cast figures, *Transcendence,* by Jack Harmon.

One further note: You may obtain brochures from the botanical gardens department; in summer, too, you may join a conducted garden tour. For information, phone (604) 228-2181.

Himalayan poppies

VANCOUVER

2 UBC GARDENS (South)

Round trip 3.2 km (2 mi)
Allow 1.5 hours
Good all year, best in June

If you enjoyed your tour of the gardens at the north end of the university campus, you will surely delight in the variety offered by the Main and Asian gardens. They are located just west of the university stadium on either side of Marine Drive a little to the north of the West 16th Avenue traffic light, though there is no direct access to the gardens from either road. The easiest vehicle approach is to turn east off Marine Drive and make a short swing to the right which takes you to parking just across the road from the garden entrance; its handsome visitor centre is a short distance beyond.

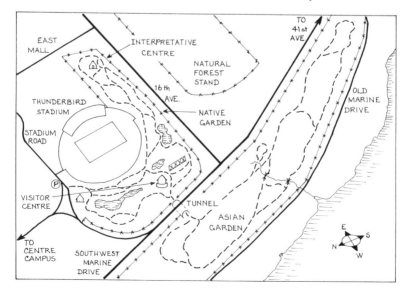

Arbor Garden

The slope down from the stadium has been landscaped to make the alpine garden, named after the collection's donor, E. H. Lohbrunner of Victoria. The garden contains representative plants of the world's various mountain regions. As you travel east, keeping the stadium fence above you on your left, you have the choice of several trails (named for local notables) into the B.C. Native Garden, a collection of indigenous plants, shrubs, and trees in typical settings, including those of the semiarid interior.

Returning westwards, you find yourself amid various examples of formal garden architecture, with walks and arbours, part being the re-creation of an old-fashioned physick garden. In this section, too, is the contemporary garden as well as other sections that are still in the evolutionary stage.

But where's the Asian Garden? For it, you must descend into a tunnel west of the arbours, one that takes you beneath Marine Drive and into an entirely different world of tall trees, massed rhododendrons and magnolias, plus a variety of exotic shrubs and climbing vines. It is a wonderful place for hot-day walking; in season its shady paths are abloom with a profusion of primulas, Himalayan blue poppy, and Asiatic dogwood and thus it is not hard to imagine yourself in some forest of Nepal. In fact, you may well feel disinclined to reverse the process and return via your subterranean route to the workaday world, even if that return takes place gradually as you complete your garden circuit, going north via the little lake and paying your final respects to the select flowers at the main gate.

For admission information, call 228-4208 except on Thursdays when admission is free.

3 POINT GREY

Round trip 12.4 km (7.7 mi)
Allow 4 hours
Beach and forest trails
Good all year

Here is a delightful circuit that may be shorter or longer according to your inclination. Nor need you retrace your steps unless you wish to, thanks to various trails connecting the beach with the cliff top near UBC. Your starting point is the farthest west parking area of Spanish Banks where N.W. Marine Drive begins its rise towards the university. (The Spanish Banks bus terminal is some twenty minutes to the east.)

First you wander along the beach, then after about twenty-five minutes, by an old searchlight tower, comes the first trail, the ascent of which, with a turn left on top, gives you a short circular tour. If you stay on the beach, you see evidence of recent attempts to halt cliff erosion as you make for a second wartime installation like the first, then round the point for your first sight of the Fraser River's North Arm breakwater. Here you have a second flight of steps, this one giving access to a point just south of UBC's Museum of Anthropology.

To complete this circuit of 6.4 km (4 mi), go left along the track seawards of the museum, and proceed via a one-time section of Marine Drive to its intersection with the present thoroughfare, then take the same route as did

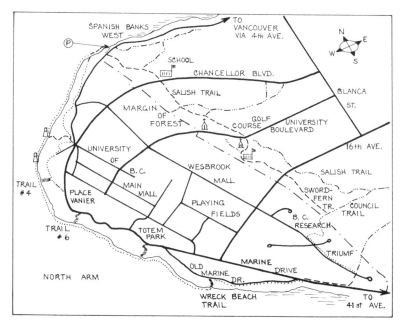

Tower at Point Grey

the shorter walk. If you wish to proceed farther still along the beach, you should check that tides are suitable and be careful to stay with the trail— here somewhat muddy—that runs along the foot of the now heavily treed slopes. Ignore the next two routes upwards (unless you do not mind walking along a busy road); go on to the original Wreck Beach Trail, its lower end located by a large rock.

Ascend this path to a recently abandoned section of Marine Drive. Go right and follow it as it heads east towards the new dual carriageway, passing an interesting viewpoint en route. Stay with the new road briefly till you see a bus stop sign on the opposite side. Scurry across here and plunge into the quietness beyond the fence. Go left at an intersection and follow the road past TRIUMF (Tri-Universities Meson Facility) till you reach the B.C. Research installation. Go right here and make for the meadow behind to find the beginning of Council Trail at the edge of the forest.

From this track turn left on what you discover is Swordfern Trail when you come to West 16th Avenue. Cross this highway and continue north, traversing two power lines as you proceed via University Hill Secondary School. Just beyond, pick up a trail heading right along its playing fields and emerge by a church on University Boulevard. Cross this thoroughfare as well and take the trail parallelling the golf course on its west side. Continue to Chancellor Boulevard and the elementary school just to the north. Stay left of its buildings and take yet another woodland trail that lies along the right-hand edge of a quite impressive ravine. By following this route, you find yourself back at N.W. Marine Drive close to your starting point, after an outing that certainly does not lack variety.

North Shore mountains across English Bay

VANCOUVER

4 CHANCELLOR WOODS

Longer circuit 6 km (3.7 mi)
Allow 2 hours
Forest trails
Good much of year

The northern segment of UBC Endowment Lands—extending from Chancellor Boulevard to Spanish Banks—contains a number of trails, mostly in forest. There is, however, considerable variety of tree cover, some quite deep ravines, and the beach if you want an alternative route for part of the way.

The trail system lends itself to circular walks, so described here are two of them, starting from the same point and in part covering the same ground. Your indicated point of departure, the Chancellor extension of West 8th Avenue, allows you to park off a main thoroughfare; it is convenient for busses also, being only a short distance west of Blanca Loop. If driving, turn west off Blanca Street just north of the bus terminal and drive to the road's end at a large mound. Just beyond, the new Chancellor Boulevard approach from West 4th Avenue links up with the original alignment on a considerable bend. Cross here to the north side.

Now you take the track into the forest, travelling north among tall trees, second growth though they are, as the great nurse stumps of the original forest show. Thus, you proceed in the midst of cedar, Douglas-fir, and hemlock which predominates. Your trail drops a little as you advance until, after about twenty minutes, you find yourself in a field ("The Plains of Abraham") with glimpses of Burrard Inlet through the trees ahead. Cross to the seaward side and, if you do not wish to drop to the beach here, turn left to head west close to the edge of the bluffs. Next comes a deep ravine, and here is the parting of the ways; the left-hand trail gives a short outing of 3.9 km (2.4 mi) that takes about an hour, while the right-hand branch descends into the depths.

The shorter trail follows the ravine's eastern edge fairly closely, though it is forced away from the main valley by washouts here and there. As you head inland, you begin to hear traffic and you find yourself back on the boulevard some distance west of where you started. To return, you may use the pedestrian sidewalk south of the highway; an attractive alternative, however, presents itself if you take the forest trail into the woods instead. Follow this for some 300 m to a cross trail and go left. At the next fork, go left again and you are back near your point of departure.

On the longer loop, you drop into the ravine, necessitating a climb out of it again if you wish to continue on the bluffs trail, here a little overgrown. You may, however, avoid this by crossing Marine Drive and walking along the beach until the road starts going uphill. Recross here to the landward side and pick up the trail heading inland just to the left of a creek. This trail rejoins the one along the bluffs and you now proceed above the gully until you emerge by University Hill Elementary School, with Chancellor Boulevard just ahead of you.

Use the pedestrian crossing and take the trail south to its intersection with another, then go left. The path you are now on, which can be somewhat damp after wet weather, goes through scrub timber, crosses a creek, then goes into nice open forest. Here you are joined by the short-route trail and henceforth the two coincide, with the final fork left bringing you back to houses and transportation.

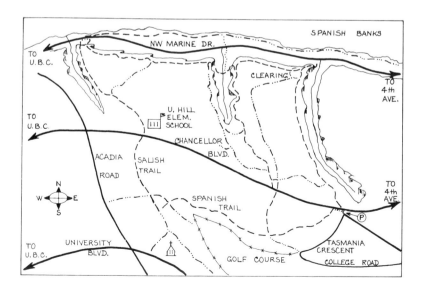

Sunshine and shadow in the forest

VANCOUVER

5 ENDOWMENT LANDS FOREST

Round trip 6.4 km (4 mi)
Allow 2 hours
Forest trails
Good much of year

As a woodland walk in UBC Endowment Lands, this circular trip should be satisfactory for the harried city dweller with a little time to spare. The only lack? Distant views to please lovers of the spectacular.

The outing begins on West 16th Avenue at the point where Tolmie Street joins it in the 4500 block. Here a built-up trail (Sasamat Trail), the result of efforts by a devoted citizen group, goes into bushland in a once-cleared area that now supports a luxuriant growth of broom, an immigrant from Britain that has established itself on Vancouver Island and in the Lower Mainland. This shrub soon gives place to small alder as you emerge by a reservoir and walk along its western edge towards a mixture of larger trees.

About ten minutes from your start, fork left at a major trail junction, and continue east, skirting an aspen grove, something of a rarity in the coastal forest zone. Next, after some thirty minutes of walking, you sense a clearing ahead as another trail (Council) joins from the right, and shortly you emerge on Imperial Trail a little south of West 29th Avenue, crossing the aptly named Tin-Can Creek to do so.

Immediately opposite is the continuation of your route, which you stay on as it first turns downhill a little and then resumes its original line, eventually emerging in an open space. Go right here on another major trail (Clinton) and head south amid some impressive second-growth timber. One word of caution, though: this track is used by horses and may be messy here and there, involving a certain amount of careful stepping.

Eventually you reach another fairly large open space just north of S.W. Marine Drive and a little west of its intersection with West 41st Avenue. Turn right here again, plunging back into the forest on Salish Trail, and travel north and west for some fifteen minutes before stepping out on Imperial once again, a considerable distance south of your original crossing and just opposite B.C. Hydro's power pole 55. Here, go left and pass the next three poles, then, just before the lane turns left and the power line goes straight ahead, cross a small creek to the right and, once more on Salish Trail, enter the woods again.

On this trail you remain, meeting Council Trail once more, till you come to a major T-junction just to the right of a footbridge. Turn right on this new path (Hemlock Trail) and proceed uphill till you arrive back at the original Y-junction just south of the reservoir. From here, simply retrace your steps to your setting-off point, your woodland outing over.

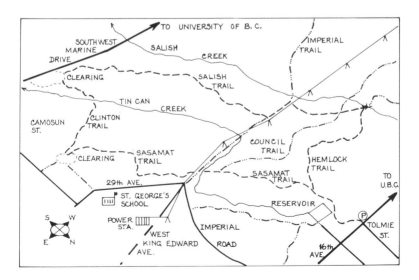

23

6 IMPERIAL TRAIL

Round trip 6.4 km (4 mi)
Allow 2 hours
Road and trails
Good all year

Among walks in UBC Endowment Lands, this one offers the greatest set of contrasts between the works of nature and those of men; from trails in deep woodland to a one-time road, now a lane, with sight of TRIUMF and B.C. Research Council installations for good measure.

One starting point for this outing is the T-junction where West King Edward Avenue meets Crown Street. From here take the track into the bush, pass the power station, and walk along a quiet residential street, treed on one side, to where West 29th Avenue becomes Imperial Road. Cross this road, noting that here is another possible beginning if you wish a shorter walk.

Your hike along the lane begins with your crossing the low wall that blocks the lane from vehicular traffic except B.C. Hydro service trucks. At first you bear a little right as you descend gently. Note, however, the trail that comes in from the right a short distance along; it should be your return route. Thereafter, as you proceed, you see one or two paths going off to the left or right; leave these aside to be explored another day and enjoy your open lane.

After the hill has eased off, lane and power line separate, and the former, your route, swings left. Now the forest round you thickens as trees on either side press in more closely, several large hemlocks looking particularly

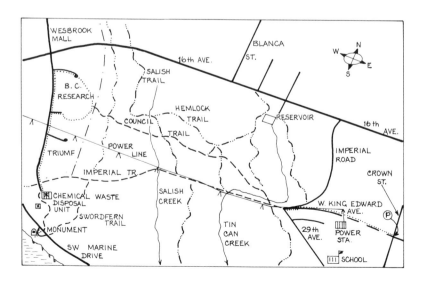

Log rafts on the North Arm

impressive. On this stretch, evidence of human interference with nature is being nicely obliterated where bush is re-establishing itself on what was blacktop not so long ago. At length, however, you go left on a signed trail (Swordfern), finally emerging into the open on S.W. Marine Drive, opposite the Musqueam historical marker that commemorates the arrival of Simon Fraser at the mouth of the river that now bears his name. By crossing the divided highway (being careful of traffic) you may enjoy the view southwest over the log-booming grounds to the deltaic lowlands and the islands of the Gulf of Georgia. Leave from the western end of the pull-out and head for a horse trail sign beside a break in the fence opposite. Follow the trail through the gap, staying left at one fork and after passing the university's chemical disposal unit, you find yourself back at Imperial. This time, however, you cross it and continue past TRIUMF (Tri-universities Meson Facility) noting on your left, en route, the hideous tar-paper building that past generations of UBC students will recognize as the old field house, once a chilly place for writing Christmas exams. Continue with the road to the buildings that house B.C. Research and make you way through these to the field behind, fronting the forest. Here, across the grass, is your return route, Council Trail.

This trail takes you through impressive second-growth timber; here great stumps yet remain of the original forest, indicating what giants were felled in the early days of B.C. logging. Stay with your trail, ignoring two or three intersecting tracks until you join a broader trail from the left, cross a creek on stepping stones, and step back on to Imperial Drive just south of the wall, ready to reverse your original approach.

One last word: If you have enjoyed these forest walks close to the city, support the efforts being made to keep this land as a provincial or regional park for future generations to enjoy.

Near Celtic shipyard

VANCOUVER

7 MUSQUEAM

Round trip 6.4 km (4 mi)
Allow 2 hours
Foot and bridle trail
Good all year

Despite its nearness to the city, this area is rich in variety, including forest, a creek, the Fraser River's North Arm, and, in open stretches, an impressive variety of wild flowers in summer, morning glory and cranesbill to name only two. Brambles also blossom profusely in summer, giving promise of luscious blackberry picking later in the year.

To enjoy these delights, park on Crown Street just south of S.W. Marine Drive and a little east of its junction with West 41st Avenue. Here you are beside Musqueam Park and across its grass you walk towards its treed western edge, where you turn roughly south on a pedestrian trail paralleling the bridle trail on your right. Proceeding through this stately forest, you cross to the left of the creek that you have been following, eventually emerging on a road (actually Crown Street after it has turned west). Go right here for a short distance, then turn left once more, this time on the bridle trail.

The next point of decision comes when you cross a large covered water main at ground level, and here again you should choose to fork half right, continuing more or less southwards, the houses of the Musqueam Indian Reserve beginning to show themselves on your right. Stay with the bridle trail as it crosses one more road (West 51st Avenue), with a deep drainage ditch on your right now separating you from Musqueam Golf Centre while

Point Grey Golf Course is to your left. On this stretch the flowers are particularly fine, many of them climbing the tall fence that separates you from the golfers. Then comes the river and another choice: go upstream or downstream or make this your destination.

Actually it matters little whether you go up or down the river. The track to your right runs along the bank parallel with Musqueam Golf Course; across the river the squat buildings of Vancouver's sewage plant on Iona Island serve as a poor substitute for the abbey of its Scottish namesake. Eventually a slough bars further progress westwards and as the land belongs to the Musqueam Indian band, you have to retrace your steps to the T-junction.

If you go left, you follow the bridle trail to its end at Carrington Street. Here you may turn right and cross a bridge to a small peninsula, its jetty allowing you a closeup view of marine traffic, both commercial and recreational, while planes from the airport to the south make their presence felt also. If you wish to explore a little farther upstream, you may follow Celtic Avenue past the shipyard and the Ministry of Forests depot, then walk along the river dyke fronting yet another golf course, McCleery.

On your return trip, you may vary the last part of your route somewhat by going right along the concrete pipe towards some playing fields. Gradually bear left round the edge of the trees to West 46th Avenue and, where it ends at Holland Street, take the little connecting lane to Crown, just where the latter changes direction. From here it is only a few steps back to your transportation and return to the city.

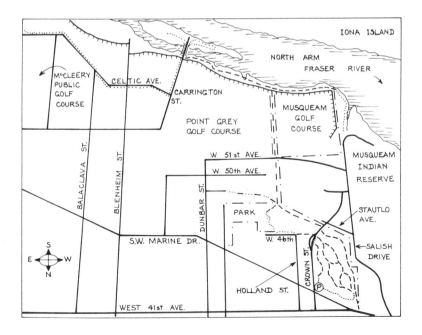

VANCOUVER

8 QUILCHENA

Round trip 4 km (2.5 mi)
Allow 1 hour
Grass and blacktop
Good all year

For those days when the weather has cleared too late for venturing far afield or when time is otherwise limited, here is an unpretentious walk within minutes of downtown. It combines charm and variety, involving as it does two parks—small ones, admittedly—and the connecting thoroughfares with their varied residential architectural features. There is even a stretch of railway thrown in for good measure.

Drive, or take the bus, along Arbutus Street to Valley Drive, the second intersection south of West King Edward Avenue; turn east here opposite the Standard gas station. Beside the white Byzantine Greek Orthodox Church (Saint George's), you see Quilchena Park right ahead where the road forks. Here is your starting point. Before setting off, however, take a little time to examine the handsome church, not only because of such features as its dome and panelled doors but also because it will serve as a landmark for your return.

The park itself, once part of a golf course of the same name but with the golf activity now confined to a small putting green, stretches ahead, rising gently to the B.C. Hydro railway that forms its eastern boundary. Stay near the northern limit of the open space as you tread turf, heading just to the left of the park keeper's house and the toilet facilities and coming onto a little tree-crowned knoll with a bench just short of the rail right-of-way. From here

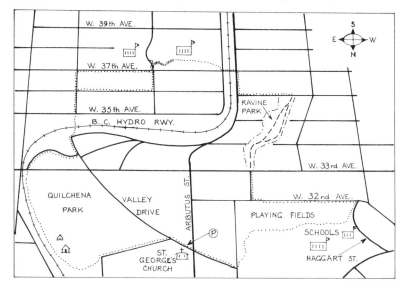

View south across Quilchena Park

you look across to the high-rise apartments of Kerrisdale and the smaller single-family dwellings of MacKenzie Heights as you continue on the grass along an avenue of fine trees, presumably a one-time fairway. On your right, grassy slopes extend down to Valley Drive, and you may want to pause at West 33rd Avenue to look back over the great sweep of Burrard Inlet and the mountains beyond.

Now your outing changes character, for the next stretch is over roads, but they are quiet roads in a residential area, so you have no worries about traffic once you cross West 33rd. First follow Quilchena Crescent, then, where it is intersected by Cypress Street, take the latter uphill by turning sharp left. At the head of the rise is a familiar sight, the railway. Cross the tracks and head uphill to West 37th Avenue. Go right here and continue to the top of the hill, at which point turn left to enjoy the view over Kerrisdale towards the Strait of Georgia from the small esplanade in front of Quilchena Elementary School.

As you continue your walk, you find that you are not yet quite finished with education, for now you descend the steps that bring you past the north façade of Point Grey Secondary School prior to your return to West 37th and your crossing of Arbutus Street. Now go one block right, then turn left on West 36th and walk about half a block to where, on the right, a stone with a plaque announces Ravine Park.

Here you turn right and begin descending the slope of this narrow sylvan corridor as the trail winds among tall trees, to emerge finally at West 33rd Avenue some distance west of your crossing on the outward trip. If you wish, you may return to Quilchena Park from here by turning right, crossing Arbutus at the lights, then going left at Valley Drive. However, a little more exploration is still possible.

Go straight forward across West 33rd and travel one more block before turning left and heading uphill between two rows of architecturally diversified dwellings to the point where you meet Haggart Street just above a children's playground and the sports fields of Prince of Wales High School. Descend diagonally across this field towards the white dome of Saint George's in the distance, aiming for a point about midway along the eastern fence where there is an opening. From this point the last little stretch of road is visible and your urban peregrination is over.

Pond in Jericho Park

VANCOUVER

 **JERICHO BEACH**

Round trip 5.4 km (3.4 mi)
Allow 2 hours
Park trail and road
Good all year

With acquisition by the Vancouver Parks and Recreation Board of the former Department of National Defence property north of West 4th Avenue between Wallace Street and Marine Drive, a whole new stretch of parkland fronting English Bay has been opened to walkers. Nor are you confined to one route: hikes of varying length are possible; even round trips along streets of stately Point Grey dwellings are feasible.

To make the most of what this area has to offer, begin not in the park proper but at the little Hastings Mill Store Museum at the end of Alma just north of where it meets Point Grey Road (the nearest bus stop is at 4th and

Alma). The unpretentious wooden building is a relic of Vancouver's earliest days: built in 1865 by Capt. Edward Stamp, it served as the first post office, community library, and recreation centre on Burrard Inlet.

Starting here, you cross little Pioneer Park and head west past the Royal Vancouver Yacht Club and Jericho Tennis Club before swinging past Brock House Senior Citizen Centre (once the Brock family home) towards the beach and a small Park Board pavilion.

From now on, you have the bay on your right and Point Atkinson and Bowen Island more or less ahead as you step, on the seaward side of a small lagoon, towards what is left of the old Jericho army base, now the Jericho Sailing Centre. Once past it, continue half left towards a grove of trees, and you come to your second pavilion at Locarno Beach.

This landmark may serve as the destination of a short walk (round trip about one hour); however, if you wish to go farther, there is nothing to stop you. Make your way, then, to Spanish Banks East with its refreshment counter and changing rooms. Here, too, you may turn round. An interesting alternative presents itself, though, if you do not wish to return by your outward route.

This continuation involves crossing Marine Drive close by the bus loop and ascending the steps up the steep bank on its landward side. These bring you out at the foot of Blanca Street, and a short walk uphill leads to Bellevue and down West 2nd, passing Aberthau, the one-time officers' mess, now a community cultural centre. From here, recross Marine Drive and return across the park, this time taking the track south of the lagoon then turning half left to reach the end of Point Grey Road once more.

A similar but slightly longer loop is available also if you continue west-wards to about halfway along the car park and ascend a flight of steps similar to that already described. This ascent brings you up to Belmont Avenue and, by turning left along it, you link up at Bellevue with the route outlined in the previous paragraph.

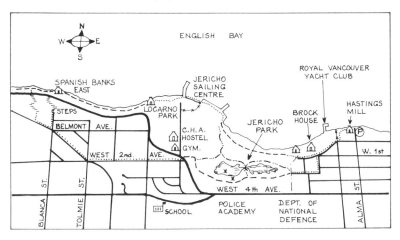

Historic railway engine

VANCOUVER

10 KITSILANO POINT

Round trip 5.1 km (3.2 mi)
Allow up to 2 hours
Path, beach, and sidewalk
Good all year

This point, the tip of the small peninsula jutting out into English Bay west of the entrance to False Creek, forms the pivot for a walk that may embrace such diverse attractions as the sight of small craft scurrying to and fro under power or sail, the tall buildings of a modern city viewed across a narrow stretch of water, museums and records of B.C.'s past, beaches, an open-air swimming pool, and a concert area; a walk that, in the bargain, covers three city parks: Vanier, Haddon, and Kitsilano.

From Cornwall Street just west of Burrard Bridge, turn north on Cypress at the traffic light and follow the Centennial Museum signs (the MacDonald bus service stops at the intersection). Though some parking is available near the marina on False Creek, space can be at a premium on a summer day. It is probably best, therefore, to use the Centennial Museum lot, noting that building's inspiring lines with their upward sweep and resolving to visit its collection some day.

First set off towards the mouth of False Creek. Have a look at the home of the city archives, the Major Matthews building, the low profile of which suggests the weight of the past in contrast to its lofty neighbour. Then come the marinas, a confusion of small craft at their slips, with the span of Burrard Bridge to the southeast providing a frame for them as well as for its more distant neighbour, Granville Bridge. Across the creek squats the new aquatic centre; fortunately it blends with its background, for it is no thing of beauty.

Now, as you head north through Vanier Park, Stanley Park begins to show itself, stretching behind English Bay, itself the anchorage for larger ocean-going ships. Behind, on the north shore, is the high country above

West Vancouver rising to the summit of Hollyburn Mountain, while farther west are the peaks round Howe Sound. On rounding this first point, too, you see closer at hand the Maritime Museum, home of the *St. Roch,* that pioneer ship of Arctic exploration, which now sits demurely above the water, sheltered from the elements that once she braved.

The museum is undergoing large-scale alterations on its seaward side, the object being to provide a breakwater jutting into English Bay, with moorings for other historic craft. In any event, carry on westwards past the building, perhaps dropping to the beach as you proceed into a small bay, one that houses an open-air swimming pool and Kitsilano Showboat, home of summer concert parties.

Here you may turn back, but you can continue westwards for another 800 m along a narrow foot trail on the seawall, passing Kitsilano Yacht Club en route. The feature of this stretch is its natural state, with a bank of wild flowers rising on the landward side. Finally, a flight of steps takes you up to a little street-end park, from which you may begin your return along Point Grey Road, quietly residential in this area.

As you return via Kitsilano Park proper, you may note the concrete slab on which C.P.R. engine 374 used to repose before its removal to a railway museum. Though it is sad to lose such a landmark, it is probably for the best since, unprotected as it was, it proved an irresistible magnet for children who favoured it over the swings and roundabouts officially installed. This time, pass the Maritime Museum on its landward side, pausing en route to examine the tall totem pole carved by Chief Mungo Martin to mark B.C.'s Centennial in 1958. Note also that you are now in Haddon Park, the name commemorating the donor of the land to the city.

To complete your return journey, use the footbridge that spans the outflow of one of the little lakes to the north of the planetarium. The actual distance covered on this hike is not great, but there is an enjoyable variety of scenery round this point, whose name commemorates a chief of the Squamish Indian band.

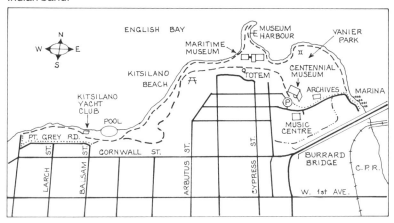

View across False Creek to the North Shore

VANCOUVER

11 FALSE CREEK

Round trip 4.8 km (3 mi)
Allow 2 hours
Paths and walkways
Good all year

Urban redevelopment over the past few years has rescued this core-city area from the blight that had settled on it, thus making it of renewed interest to walkers, providing as it does something for almost everyone— from a children's adventure playground to theatres, from city markets to marinas, with a fine stretch of creek wall thrown in. You may even make the approach a novelty if, instead of driving into the area from West 6th Avenue at the Charleson Park entry (where there is a bus loop and parking lot), you park at West 7th and Laurel and enter via the pedestrian overpass from the northwest corner of that intersection.

By so doing, you arrive at the development's highest point, the top of an attractive Japanese-type garden overlooking the whole area. Here you have at your feet water flowing to a placid lake, the haunt of ducks and swans, part of the city's Charleson Park. And the views beyond are even more striking, with the stark landscape of the inner city looming across the creek and set against a backdrop of the North Shore mountains.

Once you have gazed your fill, go to your right towards Moberley development, then, having descended to roadway level, follow signs for the Trestle Restaurant. By so doing, you emerge via Leg-in-Boot Square on the walkway by the main creek and your route from here follows it northwest as it pursues its sinuous course towards Burrard Inlet. As you proceed, you may be interested in comparing the dwellings in one enclave with those of another and savouring the clusters of road names that commemorate the industries once located here, terms from sawmilling and ironworking being well represented. Keep an eye open, all the same, for a footbridge to the right that takes you onto Granville Island proper from the west end of Charleson Park.

Once on the island, you travel back east a short way, round a small promontory, then resume walking in your original direction. Your next talking point is the cluster of floating homes called Sea Village, which comes as a prelude to the focus of activity represented by the Granville Island market. Here are stands for the sale of fruit, vegetables, and other produce juxtaposed with restaurants and cafes, all tempting you to linger a little longer before your return trip.

On your way back, either follow your original route or, having made a circuit of the one-time island, rejoin it at the bridge and retrace your steps past the residential area before heading uphill to the overpass.

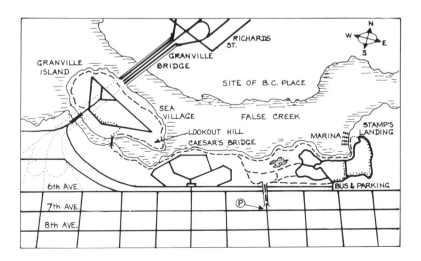

By Lost Lagoon

VANCOUVER

12 STANLEY PARK

Round trip 8 km (5 mi)
Allow 3 hours
Mostly park trails
Good all year

For a circuit embracing a number of different surroundings while keeping clear of other users as much as possible, try this walk. It begins in the park's southwest corner from one of the parking lots located close to the Park Board offices just north of Lagoon Drive or, if you are coming by bus, from the Denman Street terminal of the No. 5 or No. 8 service.

From here, make for the seawall to sample one of its most picturesque sections, the one running north along the shore of English Bay past Second Beach. At the same time, you surely do not wish to plod mechanically round the whole length of this walk, crowded as it is with pedestrians as well as cyclists. For this reason, ascend the steps at Ferguson Point to emerge on top of the low cliff opposite the Teahouse Restaurant. Stay close to the walk's edge, keeping the sea on your left as far as possible, a rule to follow on the whole of this stretch to Prospect Point.

The first point of interest is the roughly hewn stone monument to Pauline Johnson, who loved the park, gave Lost Lagoon its name, and was thus commemorated following her death in 1913. Having paid your respects to her, continue along the sidewalk of the access to the Third Beach parking lot. At the beach, remain on the land side of the pavilion and pick up the Merilees Trail, which runs along the top of the cliffs. From this trail, various viewpoints give glimpses across the bay and over to Point Atkinson and Bowen Island. Particularly spectacular is Siwash Rock, seen from the old coast defence platform that now serves as a lookout point; you may even see a cormorant perched on the rock if the seawall walk is quiet.

Past the rock, stay with the trail as it works its way round to the northeast in a forest of Douglas-fir, cedar, and hemlock, finally rising via a flight of steps to a higher level and eventually coming out at Stanley Park Drive a little south of Prospect Point. Even now, you have no need to pound the sidewalk; cross the road and follow a trail north through the bush to emerge opposite the cafe. Here you may pause either for refreshments or to look down at First Narrows or to examine the walking beam of the old S.S. *Beaver* or to contemplate the basalt dyke that helped create the headland by preventing erosion.

To resume your circuit, you may drop down from the point to the sea-level pedestrian walkway, staying with it until you reach Ravine Trail. A right turn here takes you to Beaver Lake with the choice, when you arrive there, of staying right and and going round it, or forking left along its east and south sides to another left fork where the other route links up again.

If, after Prospect Point, you cross the bridge over the causeway leading to Lions Gate Bridge, you may still drop down by staying left. Alternatively you may cross to the south side of the roadway, follow a trail south that intersects two connections with the highway, and pick up a road giving access to a works area and the other end of Ravine Trail. Continue south on this path and you find yourself at the western end of Beaver Lake with a right fork taking you to the intersection mentioned in the previous paragraph.

The last stretch of your exploring trip takes you past the park works yard to the rose garden and the underpass that brings you out on the shores of Lost Lagoon. The most rewarding route back is along the lagoon's north side, from which you see the buildings of the West End at a respectable distance in the intervals of enjoying the variety of birdlife that haunts its banks and waters.

Your outing ends with a crossing of the lagoon's westward extension and a return to your original parking area.

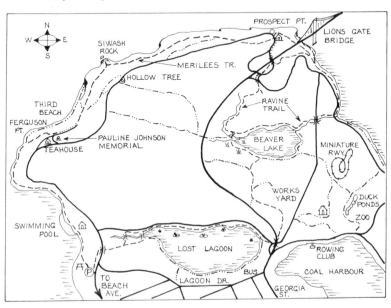

WEST VANCOUVER

13 WHYTE ISLAND

Round trip 6.5 km (4 mi)
Allow 3 hours
High point 76 m (250 ft)
Forest path, beach, and rock
Good all year (but watch the tide)

Though this rocky knoll is island by courtesy only, being accessible on foot via a boulder causeway when the tide is suitable, it makes a satisfying destination for a walk that includes a rocky spine of land overlooking Howe Sound, a pleasant little seaside park, a small-boat marina, and a beach. Of course, you can drive to Whytecliff Park, but doing so cuts the walk in two and is not nearly so rewarding.

Travelling west from the city along the Upper Levels Highway through West Vancouver, take the Squamish fork at Horseshoe Bay junction. Almost at once, however, turn left and cross the overpass, following the signs for Marine Drive. From the "Stop" sign a little way beyond, go straight ahead for just over 800 m to Hycroft Road, the second turnoff on the right. Undeterred by the "Dead End" sign, take this road and very shortly go left uphill to the road end in a small circular patch. Ahead, among the trees, lies the trail. One warning, though: parking space is limited; be sure not to block a driveway.

Once in the trees the trail forks. It does not matter greatly which one you take, however, as the trails reunite later; perhaps the one to the right is best saved for your return because of its spectacular views of the Howe Sound mountains. In any case, you can enjoy the mixture of trees—conifers and arbutus predominating—as you wander along the ridge with its rocky little viewpoints to the right.

At its western end, the trail descends quite steeply by a flight of steps to emerge on the overflow parking lot for Whytecliff Park, located just across Cliff Road. Cross the road and go down Rockland Wynd, then left along Arbutus Road, at the end of which a gate gives entry to the park. Once inside, head for the ornamental viewpoint where you will want to linger a little to enjoy the outlook over Howe Sound before continuing to the objective. To do so, walk along the rocky cliffs, cutting back inland a little to avoid an isolated promontory, then descending by a track and stone steps to the marina wharf and its wooden jetty, once a pier of the old Union Steamship Company, which ran ferries from this point.

Pass along the landward side of the mooring slips and head along the shingle beach, one frequented by skin divers in the open season, which happens to be winter (diving is banned between April 1 and October 31). At the far end of the beach is the causeway, a little slippery perhaps, but easily negotiable with care by anyone who is properly shod. The same caution applies to the island rock, though it is not too steep; ten minutes or so puts you on the summit so that you may say like another celebrated islander (Robinson Crusoe), "I am monarch of all I survey," and such a survey is rewarding. Point Grey looms across the inlet southwards, Bowen Island is to the west, and Howe Sound stretches north. And don't forget to look up from the rocky shores of Batchelor Bay to the bold headland of Eagle Bluff on Black Mountain.

To return, you may follow the same route exactly or vary it by walking directly up from the beach into the park's grassy area, stretching diagonally to reach the overflow car park in the northeast corner. And, of course, you take the other route back along Panorama Ridge, probably stopping often to admire the majestic peaks. Just one point though: don't bring Fido. No dogs are allowed in the park.

Incidentally, if you are wondering about the "y" in Whytecliff, it commemorates a long-dead land promoter named Colonel Whyte. The colonel induced the old Pacific Great Eastern Railway to spell the name of the station this way rather than following the standard spelling, which the British Admiralty survey had given to White Cliff Point because of its light-coloured granite rock.

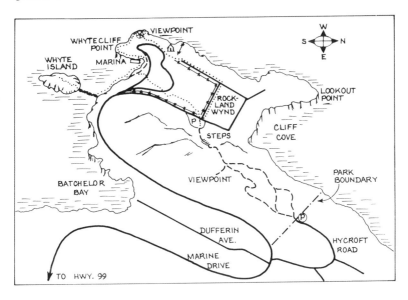

WEST VANCOUVER

14 POINT ATKINSON

Round trip (long loop)
(9.6 km) (6 mi)
Allow 3 hours
High point 122 m (390 ft)
Park trails
Good all year

Even the urban troglodytes who emerge only infrequently from the built-up sections of Vancouver must be aware of this landmark where the waters of Howe Sound mingle with those of Burrard Inlet, if for no other reasons than that its lighthouse sends friendly beams of light over the waters during the hours of darkness and its foghorn bellows its warning during periods of gloomy overcast. But Point Atkinson is well worth a visit for its own sake, located as it is at the southern tip of Lighthouse Park, which features a mixture of coastal forest, rocky headlands, and narrow bays, and is the haunt of varied wildlife, from the humble organisms of the intertidal zone to majestic birds.

To reach the park, drive west along Marine Drive from the north end of Lions Gate Bridge for a distance of just over 9.6 km (6 mi). A little past Caulfeild, after a short rise in the road, Beacon Lane lies on the left. Turn and follow it about 400 m to a designated parking area, at the end of which a gate bars further progress though a service road does continue beyond it. If possible, park a little north of the gate, close to the big information signboard on the right as you enter. This points to a main trail that goes off through tall conifers towards the northwest.

Very shortly comes the first stop: a viewpoint just to the right of the trail where large, rough-looking nests in the forks of trees are visible. These are the homes of the bald eagles, those birds that mate for life and return year after year to the same habitation, carrying out repairs and additions as needed. After this break, stay with the left fork where the trail soon branches; then, at the next divergence, go right and descend gradually to an attractive cove with dykes of igneous rock penetrating the granite and contrasting with it. A little farther south, another short diversion right, marked with a signpost, leads to Jackpine Point giving views across to Bowen Island and exhibiting all the beauty of a combined marine and forest landscape in the surroundings. Here, note the grooves in the rock, mute evidence of past glaciation.

As the trail turns southeastwards towards the point, you have your first sight of the white lighthouse tower rising among the trees. Do not make directly for it, however. It is surrounded by a high fence, and the rock rising outside is steep and may be slippery. Instead, stay on the trail as it rises to the top of the rock, emerging into the open beside the historic cairn describing the naming of the point and the history of its beacon, now in its second century, though the present tower dates only from 1912. Also recorded is the birth here of the first white child on the North Shore.

For your journey back, take the footpath to the right of, and virtually parallel to, the service road—that is if you do not succumb to the lure of the various diversions that can postpone the inevitable return to the world of men. The first of these is a short fork right to Arbutus Knoll, a rounded bluff overlooking Starboat Cove, a deep indentation that those with time and energy scramble down to. Rejoining your trail, you may continue straight back from here for a round trip of 5 km (3.1 mi); if, however, you do not mind almost doubling the length of your walk, you may follow the next minor trail to the right. This takes you first east and then north to a viewpoint overlooking Caulfeild Cove, passing en route various interesting geological features such as potholes in the granite.

As you work back west from here, you pass another short diversionary trail on the left, this one leading to the park's high point. Eventually, however, you rejoin the shorter loop just before the parking lot after what should have been a highly satisfying outing.

In passing, it may be recorded that the West Vancouver Parks Board has provided information signs along the trails, identifying a variety of natural features. The serious naturalist, though, will want to consult *Nature West Coast*, an exhaustive study of the park compiled by the Vancouver Natural History Society. Thus armed, virtually nothing can escape your identification.

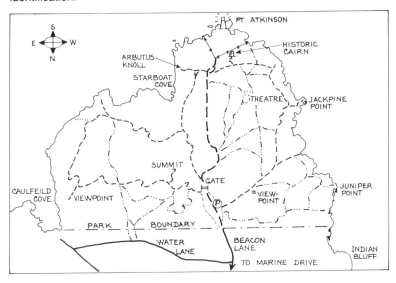

WEST VANCOUVER

15 AMBLESIDE

Round trip 6.4 km (4 mi)
Allow 2 hours
Mainly footpaths
Good all year

What Stanley Park is to residents of Vancouver, Ambleside Park is to West Vancouverites, providing a wide range of outdoor activities and catering to varied interests. Its entrance is at the seaward end of 13th Street, reached by turning onto it at its intersection with Marine Drive west of Park Royal Shopping Centre. Cross the B.C. Railway and park, preferably facing English Bay, just at the seawall walkway. On this walk, go eastwards heading towards the great natural mural that has Vancouver Harbour framed in the wide span of Lions Gate Bridge. On your left are playing fields and a swimming pool and to your right is the main shipping track through First Narrows, with Prospect Point standing guard.

Close at hand there is much to enjoy: beachcombing; feeding wildfowl in the pools that are a feature of the garden between the park road and the little public golf course; and, farther round, turning out on the fitness circuit and exercise stations. Soon, however, the east-west line begins to give way to a northeast-southwest axis as you approach the mouth of the Capilano River. Thus you turn your back on the view of English Bay and look instead towards the great heave of Crown Mountain, or closer at hand, at the dark tower that marks the southeast extremity of Park Royal and overlooks the waters of the Capilano River.

Once past the B.C. Railway underpass briefly follow the trail through the bush, then bear right again towards the river south of the Hudson's Bay store. Just as it appears that your further progress is blocked by the dark tower, a narrow passage between it and the river opens up with yet another underpass, this one of the Diarmid Guinness Bridge, completed only in 1978

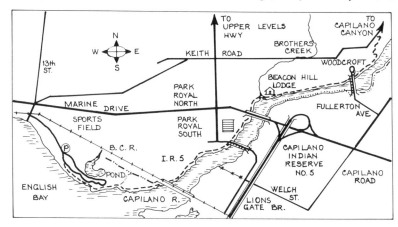

Breakers, English Bay

and linking North Vancouver with the shopping centre. Stay with the river-bank to negotiate yet a third underpass, this time of the twin bridges that carry Marine Drive traffic across the river.

From here, walk upstream, noting how the Capilano during much of the year shows the effects of the Cleveland Dam on its flow, for the river by no means fills its stream bed; its shallows are the haunts of great numbers of birds, notably crows and gulls, with both congregations keeping up a continuous chatter. This stretch, in fact, is bedlam during the salmon run, which the salmon hatchery upstream has done so much to restore.

Next comes the crossing of Brothers Creek at Beacon Hill Lodge and continuation of your expedition towards the high-rise apartments of Wood-croft Estate. Approaching these, you see yet another bridge, this one carrying traffic from North Vancouver to the development. Here, you may cross the river and return along its east bank, if you do not mind a little boulder-hopping, again negotiating underpasses but this time turning sharp left up the bank after the Guinness bridge to recross it and retrace your steps to the park and the walk along English Bay.

For a really long walk stretching to 16 km (10 mi), continue beyond Fuller-ton Bridge on the west-side trail to its junction with Keith Road. Here you turn right and, passing beneath the Upper Levels Highway, pick up the Capilano Canyon walk, which is described next.

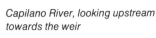
Capilano River, looking upstream towards the weir

WEST VANCOUVER

16 CAPILANO CANYON

Round trip 9 km (5.5 mi)
Allow 3 hours
Trails
Good all year

The would-be walker in this scenic valley lying between the twin municipalities of North and West Vancouver has a lengthy list of outings from which to choose, ranging from a circuit of Capilano Park itself to an interesting approach, following a one-time logging railway right-of-way, that links Keith Road in West Vancouver with Cleveland Dam.

If you wish to confine your walk to the park, drive north on Capilano Road in North Vancouver, itself reached by turning right off Lions Gate Bridge, then going left at the first traffic light. Continue straight on where Mountroyal Boulevard forks right, then go left into the dam parking area. For the alternative, however, you stay left at the bridge exit, head up Taylor Way in West Vancouver, then turn right on Keith at the first traffic light. Follow the latter road as it passes under the Upper Levels Highway and park about 400 m beyond where a locked gate bars further vehicle progress and indicates the start of your walk.

As you travel north, you pass one or two pieces of fenced-off private property on your right, one of these being the area surrounding Capilano suspension bridge. Next, after about a fifteen-minute walk, an approach from the left signals Rabbit Lane, an access route from British Properties, and here you bear a little right into the stately forest of what is now Canyon Park. Not long hereafter your trail curves into the ravine of Houlgate Creek, which on its north side offers a choice of trails, the second one to the left being perhaps the more rewarding in that it does not involve a descent followed by a subsequent climb. Finally, after passing a viewpoint of the dam on your right, you make the final ascent towards your crossing of it, your first sight of Lake Capilano being the reward for your exertions.

On your way over to the east side, you realize that your route has been joined by the Baden-Powell Trail; it, however, continues eastwards while, once across, you start the return trip downstream. Before leaving this scenic spot you will surely want to pause and admire the varied scene. Looking along the lake as it stretches northwestwards, you see the Lions, dominant on the skyline, while to your right you have the Crown Mountain massif and the whole long ridge of Grouse; the park gardens, too, are attractively laid out should you weary of the distant scene.

Now you may begin your journey back, this time using Palisades Trail, dropping down from just east of the dam via a flight of steps to reach river level at a salmon hatchery and fish weir, another spot that may detain you with its displays. Continuing downstream in the canyon itself, you may cross the bridge just below the hatchery or stay on the east bank to the river's great bend westwards. If you work your way round this, you may cross the Pipe Bridge from which you climb out of the ravine and, by staying left at successive trail junctions, you find yourself on your original out-route, just north of Houlgate Creek.

Not the least interesting feature of this walk is the sight of bald eagles, especially during the salmon run. In fact, you may imagine yourself miles from the city despite your proximity to it.

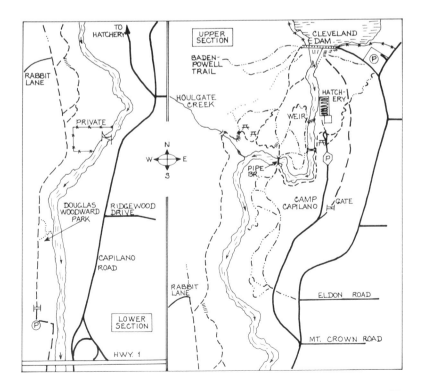

WEST VANCOUVER

17 CYPRESS CREEK

Round trip 8.8 km (5.5 mi)
Allow 3.5 hours
High point 720 m (2300 ft)
Elevation gain 500 m (1600 ft)
Park trail and service road
Good May to November

Most Vancouverites are well aware of Cypress Provincial Park. Mention of Cypress Falls Park, however, is likely to be met with an admission of ignorance despite the fact that this little gem is situated only a stone's throw from the Upper Levels Highway in West Vancouver. Hitherto it has not enjoyed—or suffered—much development, lacking even a sign at its entrance; its trails, therefore, are not overused, giving you a chance to enjoy its shade on a hot summer day within earshot of cool falling water and with closeup views of some picturesque falls.

To reach it when travelling west along the Upper Levels from Taylor Way, turn off right at the Woodgreen Drive exit, a short distance west of the highway's crossing of Cypress Creek. Stay right and go uphill to turn right once more at Woodgreen Place, a short dead-end road with limited parking by some tennis courts, part of a small playground complex. Enter the sports field and walk along its edge towards the tall conifers at its northeast corner. Here you pick up your trail heading left. This leads you gently uphill into forest, the sound of the creek becoming louder as you approach it.

After some fifteen minutes you reach the first series of falls, just above which a footbridge takes you over to the east side and a rise out of the valley

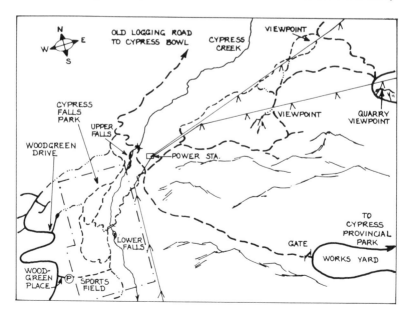

Strait of Georgia

through open forest with its stately Douglas-fir and cedar ensuring light ground cover. Note that the dampness encourages mushrooms, so the fungus collector should do well in season. Finally you become aware of power lines ahead and step out onto a service road. Turn left, ignoring a right fork that takes you towards a power station, recross the creek, go beyond the bridge for a short distance, then turn left again on an old road. To re-enter the park, go left once more on a slightly overgrown trail, which brings you back to the creek higher on the hillside, so giving you a view of the upper falls as you work back down, staying left at trail junctions until you rejoin your original route for a circuit of some 3.2 km (2 mi), the whole excursion taking over an hour.

Whereas the outing just described will satisfy many walkers, you may add both distance and altitude to this walk by turning right at the power station fork and using the B.C. Hydro service road to follow the power lines uphill, putting "a stout heart to a stey brae" as the Scots say. Stay left with the right-of-way at the next fork and, when the service road ends below a bluff, follow a foot trail upwards first on the west, then on the east, pausing from time to time to savour the developing views south over Burrard Inlet and the Strait of Georgia as you gain height.

Finally, you reach either power line 07 or 08 depending on which road you have ascended, and here, between the pylons, you take a road heading right into the forest to the east and soon emerge just below the main Cypress Parkway. Here you go right on an old road downhill which has one fine viewpoint on it to the west and south; otherwise you are in second-growth forest till you re-emerge on the power line a little above the distribution station. Once back on the road, you may complete the short circular route already described.

Morning haze over Vancouver

WEST VANCOUVER

18 LOWER HOLLYBURN

Round trip 12 km (7.5 mi)
Allow 4.5 hours
High point 953 m (3040 ft)
Elevation gain 470 m (1500 ft)
Forest trails and old roads
Good May to October

With so much activity now concentrated on Hollyburn's upper reaches, it may be forgotten that a well-established system of trails exists along its lower south-facing slopes, providing the kind of outing that is ideal for spring or fall when conditions above may be less than ideal. The half-day circuit described here is one that allows you to sample most of its features: forest, ravines, lakes, even the two privately owned lodges.

One satisfactory starting point is Hi-View Lookout, 4.7 km (3 mi) beyond the Cypress Provincial Park turnoff from the Upper Levels Highway. Park as close to the east end as you can, and cut across the corner to the upper end of the concrete dividers lining the curve. Walk a few paces right, then turn uphill. After about five minutes, take the left fork (the right one meets the Brothers Creek trail near Eyremount Drive) and continue rising in a northwesterly direction until, after another ten minutes, you meet a trail on which you go right. Quite soon thereafter you cross an old road, then a small creek in a ravine before emerging on a washed-out road, which takes you uphill to a power line that runs east and west. Just on its upper side turn sharp right. (The trail going straight on is your return route.)

Now you remain more or less with the power poles as you travel east, sometimes on the right-of-way, sometimes in open forest, sometimes in ravines and across their creeks on fragile bridges. After the fifth of these,

Lawson Creek, you find yourself at a small rest spot, and here you turn left, heading uphill for Cypress Park Resort on a section of the Baden-Powell Trail. Some thirty-five minutes along this route, a trail goes off right to Blue Gentian Lake, a possible alternative loop that avoids the lodge buildings and brings you to West Lake by a left fork from Blue Gentian. In front of the lodge, if you remain on the main trail, stay right on the rough foot track when the Baden-Powell forks left. From this route, looking over the lake, you can see the peaks of Crown and Goat standing above the trees to your right.

Now you work back left and uphill, rejoin the Baden-Powell Trail—in winter a cross-country ski route (The Grand National)—and proceed along this trail until it turns right and rises. Here, go straight on for First Lake and Hollyburn Lodge.

As soon as you have crossed the lake outlet, turn left on the hiking trail just before the forest ranger station. On this path head south, noting on either side the picturesque cabins. As you descend, you stay right at the first two forks, left at the third, but at the next one, where the road stays left and a steep narrow trail goes down right, descend by the latter to cross a dirt road just west of and below a TV relay tower. Continue to descend the foot trail, cross a very old road, and finally turn left on an eroded bit of the old logging road just above the power line. From here you are back on your original route so the rest of your walk is a simple reversal of it.

A variant of the route described is possible if you are with a two-car party. In this instance, you may leave a vehicle at the Quarry Lookout 8.8 km (5.5 mi) from the Upper Levels, then having returned to the power line, turn right instead of going downhill and follow the right-of-way. You may, in fact, make the complete circle from this alternative starting point.

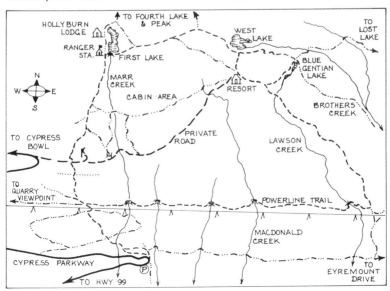

WEST VANCOUVER

19 BADEN-POWELL TRAIL
(Hollyburn Ridge)

Round trip 11.1 km (7 mi)
Allow 4.5 hours
High point 1090 m (3500 ft)
Elevation gain 270 m (850 ft)
Trail and service road
Good June to October

Use of the Baden-Powell Trail as part of its circumference permits you to undertake an interesting circular outing in the Hollyburn-Cypress area, which includes unspoiled forest and various small lakes but, alas, some man-spoiled landscape as well. Even if you do not wish to make the complete round, you may hike sections of it by judicious selection of a starting point, or by a two-car operation.

Your best point of departure is Parking Lot 5 on the west side of Cypress Parkway located about 11 km (7 mi) from its beginning at the Upper Levels Highway and a little beyond the Cypress Park Resort sign. By starting here, you get the least aesthetic part of your excursion over at the beginning when

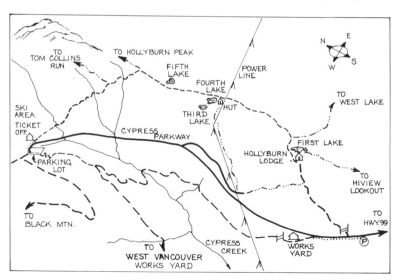

Near Hollyburn Lodge

you have to walk a short distance uphill on the road, noting as you pass the Hollyburn fire access route opposite since that will be your return. After some 200 m, turn left on the road to the park maintenance yard, walk to its northwest corner, and from there proceed via an old logging road, which makes its way up the valley of Cypress Creek.

After about thirty minutes you come to the crossing, then, having climbed out of the valley, continue right and uphill, ignoring a left fork and finally reaching the downhill ski area parking lot. Traverse this, and just across the end of the access road look for an orange diamond marker beside the ski-ticket cabin indicating the start of the trail's Hollyburn Ridge section. On this part of your journey you are in unspoiled forest, crossing interesting little creeks and climbing at first gently, but later somewhat more steeply. Stay right at the junction with the old Mount Strachan trail, now signed "To Tom Collins Run," and continue for ten minutes longer till you meet the main trail to Hollyburn Peak as you reach the ridge proper.

Stay right at this junction also, descending gently to pass the first of the little lakes that you meet on this stage of your outing. Soon you see power lines running at right angles to your route and you reach the right-of-way via one or two other small bodies of water, Fourth Lake being closest to the trail (Second and Third are a little farther west). At the warming hut, you see the main hiking trail heading southwards, en route to First Lake and Hollyburn Lodge; follow this after you have savoured the views over to Crown Mountain and southeast across the sprawling urban accretion that is Greater Vancouver.

At the lodge, you say good-bye to Baden-Powell, your route turning right behind the building and following the main service road back to the park highway. On the way, ignore a trail going off right; it leads to the cross-country ski parking lot some distance above the point at which you wish to reach the road.

WEST VANCOUVER

20 BLACK MOUNTAIN LOOP

Round trip 9 km (5.5 mi)
Allow 3 hours
High point 1250 m (4000 ft)
Elevation gain 320 m (1000 ft)
Road and trail
Best June to October

Until the late 1970s this picturesque summit and its subalpine plateau were attainable only by those prepared to ascend from just above sea level at Horseshoe Bay. Now, however, thanks to Cypress Parkway, they may be reached with a fraction of the energy required before.

Tantalus Range from the North Peak

From the downhill ski area parking lot at the road's end, go left uphill, your route's beginning identified by a Baden-Powell Trail sign and an orange square. First your track rises southwards, providing a rich variety of views over Point Grey and the Strait of Georgia, with Mount Baker rising grandly in the southeast. Next you turn sharply back, rise quite steeply for a little ways, then come to the main Black Mountain ski run. At this fork, double back left, then right again, and thus you reach the chairlift's upper terminal.

Just behind this structure, the trail strikes off west into a pretty valley. Here the loop begins. If you take the left fork, you descend a short distance south to a lake in a shallow bowl, turn west, then gradually swing round to meet the Baden-Powell Trail again just below the main summit, from which you have views from the southeast round to the sweep of the Vancouver Island peaks away to the west. To complete your loop when you have returned to the trail, continue north, then, for a striking outlook across to the Lions and the Tantalus Range, take the side trail to the North Peak, the so-called Yew Lake Lookout.

Back on the main trail, you drop once again into the valley, the north end this time, and thus you return to the chairlift for the descent to your car.

If the foregoing sounds rather strenuous, you have, from the same parking lot, an interesting short loop trail of 3.2 km (2 mi) along the shore of Yew Lake to tempt you out of your car for an hour or so. For this outing, cross the road at the comfort station and pick up your signposted route near the foot of the Mount Strachan chairlift. The trail winds, by way of the outlet creek and across meadows, to the lake with its interesting ecological features.

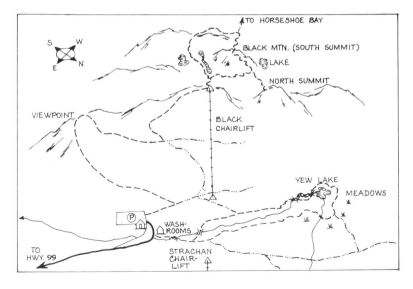

Lost Lake

WEST VANCOUVER

21 BROTHERS CREEK TRAILS

Long circuit 11.6 km (7.2 mi)
Allow 4 hours
High point 812 m (2600 ft)
Elevation gain 435 m (1400 ft)
Forest trails
Good May to November

One nice point about the trip described here is that the route's elongated shape allows you to sample slices of suitable length if you do not wish to indulge in the whole delicacy. It provides rich variety, too: maturing second-growth forest with, here and there, survivors of the original giant cedars, a creek with three sets of falls and canyons, and two forest lakes as well, if you make the longest trip.

To reach its starting point from Taylor Way's intersection with Highway 99, continue straight ahead into British Properties, turn left at the T-junction, and pick up Highland Drive at the first four-way stop. Stay on Highland until, finally, you turn left on Eyremount Drive and continue to where that thoroughfare curves back sharp right and becomes Millstream Road. Park here close to a gated forest road going off west, with orange squares indicating that it gives access to the Baden-Powell Trail. In about five minutes, turn right uphill and after another quarter-hour take the right fork signposted for Brothers Creek and Lost Lake.

A few minutes thereafter you cross a power line right-of-way, noting in passing that it is the route of the Baden-Powell Trail. Now you plunge into forest, the creek well below you on your right, and thus you remain until, after track and waterway have both levelled off, you come to the first place of choice: a footbridge with white triangle markings takes you right, over the creek, to an eventual junction with the return route, giving a round trip of 6 km (3.7 mi) for which you should allow about two hours.

If you stay left and continue up the main trail (marked with orange triangles), you have first of all a level stretch where the creek is just another pleasant forest stream, but then you rise again and soon you are viewing your first set of falls, above which you are faced with another choice: to cross the creek or not. Here again you may start your return by staying right once you have crossed on the bridge to the east bank, then descending on a fire access road, eventually linking up with the lower circuit trail for a round trip of 8.6 km (5.4 mi) and a time of nearly three hours.

For the longest walk, stay west of the creek, following red markers. Another twenty minutes or so of walking brings you to pretty little Blue Gentian Lake where there are picnic tables and, in summer, an abundance of water-lily flowers. From it, stay right, drop a little to cross a small creek, then, following signs for Lost Lake, cross Brothers Creek, just beyond which are interesting views into the gorge of the upper falls. After a half-hour walk, traverse the outlet of the lake you are seeking, another possible stopping point complete with picnic table.

On resuming your walk, follow the orange markers downhill, and after ten minutes you return to the middle bridge, but on the creek's east side. Soon your trail becomes the road mentioned earlier, and along it you march amid impressively large trees, with various stumps giving silent record of other long-gone forest giants. After some thirty minutes, the white trail joins from the west and with this you stay for about fifteen minutes till it forks left. Here you stay right and very soon thereafter reach the power line with its orange square markers. Now you must regain lost height as once more you go right, winding in and out of forest. The reward for this short climb comes when you drop to the creek just below its lower falls, a most impressive sight at spring runoff time. A short rise on the west side brings you back to the original trail junction and a left turn takes you back to British Properties.

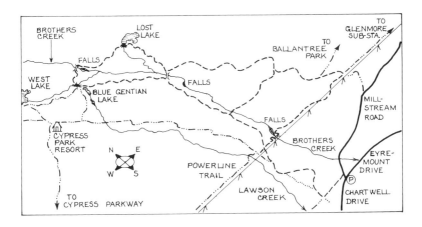

WEST VANCOUVER

22 BALLANTREE

Round trip 4 km (2.5 mi)
Allow 1.5 hours
Forest trails
Good most of the year

Looking for a short winter walk within easy reach of British Properties? Try this circular outing on the lower slopes of Hollyburn for a forest trail ending in Ballantree Park which offers an adventure playground and views across to Crown Mountain, to Grouse Mountain ski area and the north-running ridge, and over the city and inner harbour.

As with Brothers Creek, your approach through British Properties is via Highland Drive and Eyremount Drive. This time, however, turn right off Eyremount onto Crestline Road, which you follow to its junction with Millstream. Park there a little before the Glenmore power station, then ascend the power line westwards, noting that it carries the familiar Baden-Powell Trail markings. Ignore the first intersecting trail, which you reach after about ten minutes, but do go right on the forest access road some fifteen minutes later.

On this road you do not remain long, turning right again on a forest trail with white markers that takes you north and east towards the watershed boundary. Finally, however, you come down off the trail into an open space, part of the park, and with the trail sign behind you, turn right again over a bridge and keep working to the right to cross a clearing, prior to picking up a trail again that runs southwards above the houses on the west side of Ballantree Drive itself.

The route you are following brings you out at the end of Kildonan Road and a short walk along it returns you to your parking spot. Incidentally, given that most of the street names have a Scottish flavour, it looks as though

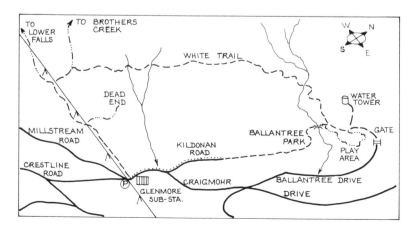

Skunk cabbage

"Ballantree" were a slightly distorted version of "Ballantrae," the setting of Robert Louis Stevenson's historical romance.

Another and more practical point: Since this walk abuts on the Brothers Creek one (Hike 21), you may combine parts of that outing with the trail just described. For example, go up to the lower falls, turn right on the west-side trail, recross at the first junction, and follow the complete set of white markers back to the park.

Deer browsing

NORTH VANCOUVER

23 BADEN-POWELL TRAIL
(Grouse Mountain)

Round trip 4.8 km (3 mi)
Allow 2 hours
High point 530 m (1700 ft)
Elevation gain 280 m (900 ft)
Forest trail and power line
    right-of-way
Good most of the year

This makes a nice walk for winter or spring, but since a good half of it is through forest, it is not unsuitable for a summer outing also, especially if you organize it so you do any climbing on one of its shaded stretches. In fact, because your route is roughly banana shaped, you may start either from the Grouse Mountain Skyride or from Skyline Drive, which leads to the disused chairlift; in addition, you may begin along the B.C. Hydro power line right-of-way and return via the Baden-Powell Trail, or vice versa.

For the eastern end of this walk in North Vancouver, turn right off Capilano Road onto Mountroyal Boulevard. From the latter go uphill on Skyline Drive to park by the power line. To travel west on the right-of-way, simply take off, enjoying views of Burrard Inlet and later the East and West Lions as you descend a little in your progress. When you reach the overflow parking for the Skyride, look carefully uphill for your return route at its western end just before the approach road, Nancy Greene Way. You should see the trail going up into an alder thicket, within which is its sign just on the edge of the true forest.

Now you do gain height but in nice open woodland on a well-graded trail, furnished with wooden walkways and steps at difficult spots. You have views, too, from time to time when the trees open out and you look south and east over Burrard Inlet to the city and beyond. Nor need you worry about decisions; only one reverse fork breaks your otherwise uninterrupted progress. As you near Skyline Drive, however, you do have a fork to take account of, the trail to the left being the official one, emerging at the one-time chairlift parking lot, the other bringing you to the road just west of it. Either way, you walk downhill to your waiting car two bends below.

Obviously, you may start from the opposite end by driving straight up Capilano Road to Nancy Greene Way and heading for the Skyride's lower terminal. This time, you see the overflow parking on your right a little below the installation, its west end providing access to the already described trail.

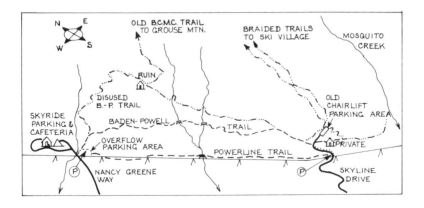

NORTH VANCOUVER

24 MOSQUITO CREEK

Round trip 4 km (2.5 mi)
Allow 2 hours
High point 520 m (1675 ft)
Elevation gain 160 m (500 ft)
Forest trail and power line
    right-of-way
Good most of the year

This short walk has something to suit almost any taste: a stretch of forest, an open track along a power line, and the creek which had a footbridge erected by Boy Scouts as part of a Centennial project. It is close in, too, so it makes a perfect outing for a short winter day or for an afternoon at almost any other time of year.

Besides the power line right-of-way and the Baden-Powell Trail, the route makes use of part of the Saint George's Trail, which links the Upper Lonsdale area of North Vancouver with the old Grouse Mountain Highway and for hardy outdoors types provides access to Mount Fromme and Thunderbird Ridge. Reaching your departure point is a trifle complicated, so follow these directions with care. Drive up Lonsdale to Osborne, turn right for one block, go left on Saint George's to Balmoral, right again here for one more block, then left on Saint Mary's. All is now plain sailing. Drive to the top of Saint Mary's even where it narrows and becomes steep, and park in the cleared space by the power line to the left of the road.

Looking due west, you see the track running along the right-of-way with another coming downhill at an angle from the right. Note this in passing: you will descend it on your return route. Now follow your nose in the direction of the distant summits of Hollyburn and Strachan, pausing, though, to enjoy the view over city and harbour from above. The farther you proceed, the more you become aware of houses and gardens below on the left; finally you see a road angling across towards you. Descend to the road and walk right towards two large green water towers close to the bank of Mosquito Creek. As you near them, you see the markers of the Baden-Powell Trail

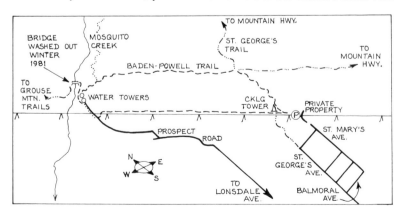

Original footbridge over Mosquito Creek

pointing upstream. At the same time, another part of the trail, visible just behind the towers, descends the hillside from the right. This will be part of your return route, but first take a short walk alongside the creek to the site of the footbridge. Here the water descends, splashing over large stones in a setting that is so utterly peaceful that you could be miles from the nearest dwelling instead of on the outskirts of a large city.

Retrace your steps to the trail where it ascends behind the water towers. The grade remains reasonably gentle and you are now among trees that provide welcome shade on a warm day. This is the sylvan part of your walk, and though the forest consists of second-growth timber, its trees are sufficiently impressive. In spring, too, the open banks are clothed with yellow violets, giving a touch of colour. As you progress, you may also applaud the industry and ingenuity of the Scouts in bridging small creeks and in building steps to aid upward progress.

Finally you reach a trail junction. Ahead of you the Baden-Powell Trail continues eastwards to emerge eventually on Grouse Mountain Highway, but at right angles to it and running up and down the slope is Saint George's Trail. Go right (downhill) on this trail and in a few minutes you see a tall radio mast (CKLG). Next you come on a dirt road angling downhill from the wired enclosure, and following this soon brings you in sight of the power line and your car.

NORTH VANCOUVER

25 LYNN CANYON

Round trip about 6.5 km (4 mi)
Allow 3 hours
Forest path and park trail
Good all year

This beauty spot is so popular, especially on summer weekends, that many visitors are unable to make the most of its varied attractions because of car parking difficulties and the press of numbers in the central area near the suspension bridge. The walk described here avoids the worst of the crowds while still allowing you to visit the main points of interest in a reasonably energetic walk that includes less frequented sections of this miniature wilderness.

To reach its starting point from Vancouver, go north across Second Narrows Bridge and take the second exit right off Highway 1. Follow the signs for Lillooet Road and travel on it as it rises between rows of timber townhouses. Continue upwards past the signs for Capilano College and through North Vancouver Cemetery, staying with the road as it narrows and becomes an unsurfaced private thoroughfare (still open to the public, however). About 3 km (2 mi) from the turnoff, a large Centennial Trail sign on the right announces the starting point of your walk from the opposite side. Some parking is available a little farther up the road on the left, so you should walk back from there.

Take the path that drops off westwards, following the orange markings. This soon levels off and traverses open forest along a high bench that allows glimpses of Lynn Creek far below. Though the descent, when it

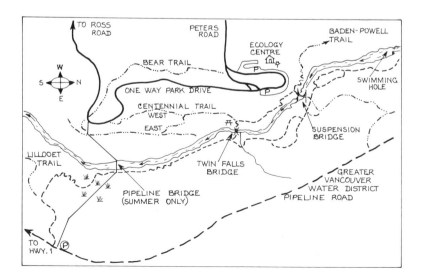

Lynn Canyon suspension bridge

comes, may seem steep, the trail is nicely graded and you soon find your-self down by the stream. Once on the valley bottom, your route travels over a wooden footway across a marshy stretch where a main pipe traverses the creek, allowing for a possible summer crossing when the water level is low.

Your main trail, however, stays on the east bank, rising gradually as the valley walls converge and steepen. Finally, after ascending a flight of steps, you come to the first bridge crossing, Twin Falls, a lovely, dark, mysterious spot where the stream is pent in its miniature canyon. The route from the west bank approaches the footbridge down a steep flight of steps. Here you may cross, turn right, and continue upstream, keeping a watch out for the first sight of the suspension bridge.

Once you see it, you are close to the park centre. The main drive with its parking is on the left, the refreshment concession is straight ahead, and a little way up the road is the Ecology Centre where both eye and ear are catered to through varied displays. In front of the centre is a metal sculpture called *Life on the Land* by Bruce F. Pearson.

Now it is time to approach the suspension bridge. Before crossing, how-ever, note that it is also used by the Baden-Powell Trail, coming down-stream to this point on the west bank and here swinging over to the other side. Once over, follow the orange markers; they are guides to your return route. Before turning south, though, check the trail to the left, which leads in a short distance to a clear pool, popular for summer swimming.

Returning from your side trip, you set off downstream again, perhaps lingering at the various viewpoints that allow glimpses of the creek, its falls, rapids, and clear pools. All too soon, however, comes the Twin Falls cross-ing once more, after which your route descends to creek level before taking you back uphill to your point of departure.

The historic mushroom

NORTH VANCOUVER

26 HISTORIC MUSHROOM

Round trip (to viewpoint) 6.8 km (4.2 mi)
Allow 3.5 hours
High point 595 m (1900 ft)
Elevation gain 458 m (1500 ft)
Trail
Good most of the year

To the older generation of outdoors people, this name will conjure up memories of the days when vehicle access to Mount Seymour ended at the 500-m (1600-ft) level and further progress was on foot, a far cry from today's highway, which takes its speeding cars to over 1000 m (3200 ft). For your approach, a particularly appealing one, you may use yet another stretch of the Baden-Powell Trail to take you from the suburbia of North Vancouver up the western flank of Mount Seymour, first following a gentle creek where you can hear the silence, then climbing steadily through open forest.

You reach the starting point from the Deep Cove exit off Second Narrows Bridge by following the park sign left after crossing the Seymour River on Riverside Drive, going right on Mount Seymour Parkway, then turning left on Berkley Road. This you drive for 2 km (1.2 mi) to a T-junction with Hyannis Drive. Go left and the trailhead is a few metres along on the north side.

You have forest and creek for companions as you head upstream, first on the west bank, then over a small footbridge to the east. After about thirty minutes ignore an unmarked trail that comes in from the right: instead stay with the orange markers as the grade steepens and you begin your climb out of the little glen, still amid trees, however. The next noteworthy feature is a power line to your left with a trail leading to it. Keep this in mind for a possible return to your route should you choose to come back via the right-of-way; meanwhile, however, stay in the forest, climbing steadily and remaining untroubled by the sun.

At last you come to a trail junction and a sign pointing you left to the Historic Mushroom. Now you do cross the power line, but almost immediately you plunge into forest again on its north side for the rest of your trip into the past: to the one-time parking lot, now partly overgrown; the large stump, no longer with the little shelter on top that gave it a name, remaining as a mute memento of the days when it served as a notice board and rendezvous. From here, you may return to the power line for your trip back, a total distance of 6.4 km (4 mi), but if you want a little more exercise coupled with a view over the city, follow Blair Range Trail. It continues upwards from the right of the stump to reach the present-day highway 800 m beyond and above the one-time meeting place.

Returning from your viewpoint, continue straight on instead of going right at the trail junction a short distance below the highway. By so doing, you drop directly to the power line and a turn to the right on this right-of-way soon brings you back to your original crossing point. From here, especially if the day is clear, you may want to remain on the service road as it winds downwards, at first gently, then somewhat more steeply, giving you two hairpin bends to negotiate before you look for the track back into the woods at the most southerly point of the lower of these turns. This spot is marked at present by a small cairn, tape, and one of the original orange triangular Baden-Powell markers.

Back on your trail, you simply retrace your steps to enjoy once more the peace of the forest. Take care, however, to go right at that unmarked trail junction shortly before you recross the creek.

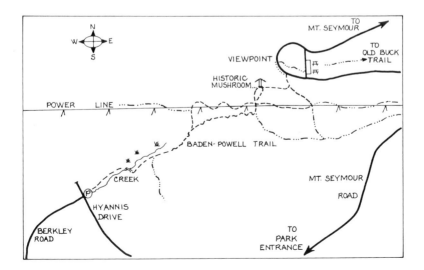

27 BADEN-POWELL TRAIL (Mount Seymour)

Long round trip 6.4 km (4 mi)
Allow 2.5 hours
High point 500 m (1600 ft)
Elevation gain 281 m (900 ft)
Trail and power line right-of-way
Good most of the year

Those who have driven the highway in Mount Seymour Provincial Park must be aware of the large wooden archway on the west side of the road just below the power line right-of-way. The stretch of trail thus announced provides a pleasant woodland walk in its own right; it also gives the chance of return along the power line service road as an alternative to retracing your steps.

Drive up Mount Seymour Road for about 2.4 km (1.5 mi) from the park entrance to the small parking area and picnic site opposite the sign, cross the road, and you are on your way. At first the trail gains only a little height as it heads west; later, however, it links up with an old logging road and from now on rises steadily in open forest of the usual second-growth timber. The trees, however, are tall and well spaced, and the ground is relatively open.

Finally, through a tunnel of trees, the wires of the power line become visible and now comes the parting of the ways. A rerouting of the trail takes it off west in the forest; you, however, want to strike forward to the open right-of-way. As you reach the cleared stretch, you find that you are actually beyond the highest point and that your view is westwards over Lynn Valley to West Vancouver and out across the harbour to Point Grey in the distance.

The dirt service road is just on the upper site of the pylon so now you turn back on this road, rising at first to the high point of the ridge, then gently descending eastwards. Now your view is towards Eagle Ridge on the other side of Indian Arm. Let it be conceded that although power lines are no things of beauty, in this instance the wide swath cleared for them does provide far more extensive views than would otherwise be the case.

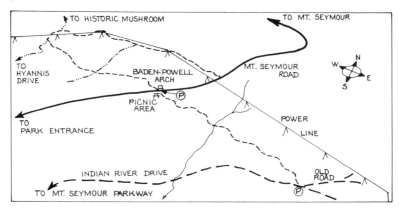

Trail sign at Mount Seymour Road

Next comes your return to the highway below the hairpin bend where it turns back on itself. The road you have followed ends just above the thoroughfare, but it is easy to scramble down from just behind the last pylon. Watch for traffic, though, as you turn towards your original starting point, the ornamental trail arch, for a round trip of 4.4 km (2.7 mi).

For any who want a longer and more invigorating walk than the described route gives, an extension is possible, which has its beginning and end not on Mount Seymour Road but on Indian River Drive below it and to the east. This route provides more interesting forest walking, again following the orange markers of the Baden-Powell Trail, and introduces you to a different section of it.

To reach the start, turn right on a gravel road bearing a "No Exit" sign, just before the park entrance and traffic light. From the turnoff, drive 3 km (1.9 mi) to where the trail goes off left on the summit of a small rise just before an old logging road. The start is none too clear, so look carefully for marker triangles. Once on it, however, you should have no difficulty as the trail winds along; wooden bridges span creeks and walkways cross marshy stretches for added convenience. The forest here is deep and cool so this trail is a pleasant outing for a warm day. Even the picnic tables by Mount Seymour Road are shady if you wish to stop there. If not, the archway already mentioned is just opposite. Thus you add 2 km (1.3 mi) to the round trip and treat yourself to an attractive piece of forest trail.

Morning mist near Goldie Lake

NORTH VANCOUVER

28 GOLDIE LAKE

Round trip 6.4 km (4 mi)
Allow 2.5 hours
High point 1000 m (3200 ft)
Elevation gain 218 m (700 ft)
Park trail and road shoulder
Good June to October

"What do you know of Seymour, who only Seymour know?" Such a question may well be asked of the many visitors to Mount Seymour Provincial Park who drive to the top parking area, inspect the downhill ski facilities around it, then depart wondering what all the fuss is about. As an interesting way of finding out more, this hike over park trails may provide an answer, taking you as it does through cool forest to a picturesque little lake situated a short distance below the level of the parking area and to the east of it.

For the start of your journey of exploration, drive Mount Seymour Road to the parking lot on the west side of the hairpin bend at km 11.1 (mi 7), the prominent "Cabin Trail" sign just before the bend being another point of identification. Cross to the highway's east side at the corner and pick up the trail as it angles off slightly downhill to bypass the lower end of a ski run. After this, the forest asserts itself and the only signs of human activity among the trees are some elderly log cabins, survivors of the days before this area acquired park status. Travelling thus, you come to a trail junction, and here you go left. Now you are on Perimeter Trail, designed, as its name suggests, for straying skiers; hence, it is clearly marked with parti-coloured diamond-shaped signs. To give the Parks Branch credit, it has carried out many improvements without making them too obvious, providing footing in soft spots and bridging creeks where necessary. The first of these, reached just after the junction, is Scott-Goldie Creek, where you may admire a miniature canyon before you continue northwards.

After an hour or so in forest, you leave the main trail as it swings right and you go left to another trail junction close to one or two small lakes. At this fork a sign points right to your objective, Goldie Lake, with the route encircling its shoreline. Your best way round it is counterclockwise, for this gives you full benefit of the area's attractions before bringing you to a trail that rises to the right and leads you via the Goldie rope tow to the top parking lot, where there are a cafe and comfort stations.

If you do not wish to retrace your steps, you may cross the parking lot and head southwards down the west side of the road, savouring the great sweep of scenery from the Gulf Islands across the Strait of Georgia to the neighbouring peaks and ridges of Burrard Inlet's north shore. Fortunately the road shoulder is wide and after some 800 m you are back in sight of your parked vehicle, so ending a trip that has put you in touch with the less public side of Mount Seymour Park.

Should the outing just described sound a little strenuous, try a shorter circuit from the top parking lot, beginning behind and just to the left of the comfort station. Follow the sign for Goldie Lake, though you may add the Flower Lake loop to your trip by going right at the first fork. This circuit of the two lakes gives you a trip of 3.6 km (2.2 mi) with no great change of elevation involved, and each lake is pleasant to linger by.

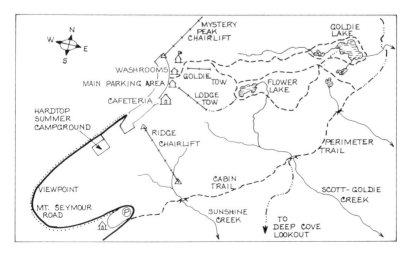

NORTH VANCOUVER

29 DOG MOUNTAIN

Round trip 8 km (5 mi)
Allow 3 hours
Trail
Good June to October

This walk, with virtually no climbing involved despite its title, takes you from the top parking area in Mount Seymour Provincial Park to a point overlooking the Seymour River, one that gives breathtaking views of Vancouver and its sister municipalities to the south and west, and Mount Garibaldi and Mamquam to the north, while Mount Baker provides a majestic backdrop to the lower Fraser Valley. The trail itself is pleasant also, lying in open forest for much of its length and broken by First Lake set in its subalpine meadow.

To start, park as close as possible to the lower chairlift terminal at the north end of the main parking area. Just left of it the main Alpine Trail heads off northwards to Mount Seymour. Follow this for a short distance, then turn sharp left en route to your own mountain, and very soon the works of man are left behind. After some twenty minutes, you reach the little lake, its name sadly uninspired in terms of its surroundings—a wooded basin with, surprisingly, a quite large cabin perched on a bluff above.

Cross at the lake outlet, noting as you do the trails that join from the right, as they can provide a variation of your return route. Again you enter forest and in it you remain until, practically at your destination, you emerge on a rocky outcrop with an almost sheer drop to the valley below. Here is the panoramic view of the features already mentioned as well as the great mass of Cathedral Mountain to the northwest and—to move from the great to the small—the remains of a cabin just in front of you, a relic of the time when the Vancouver Water District kept a lookout here.

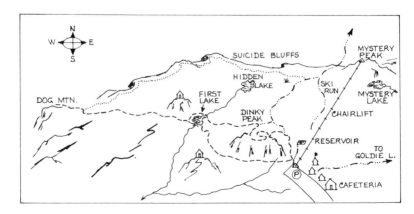

Looking northwest from Dog Mountain

When you start your return journey on the main trail you may, if you are experienced and properly equipped, and the season is summer, follow the taped route that stays left and goes straight ahead where the path turns right. This, however, winds up and down—sometimes quite steeply—over several minor summits; it is, besides, on occasion somewhat close to Suicide Bluffs for comfort, so if you decide against it but wish a slightly longer walk on your return, there is another possible variant from First Lake, with a miniature mountain, Dinkey Peak, for good measure.

At the lake outlet, then, turn left and north following the trail uphill. Gradually you veer to the east to meet a route that comes from the main Mount Seymour Trail. Go right at this fork and soon you are enjoying yet another view, this time looking south from above the car park. Thereafter, continue to the junction with the main trail at which a right turn brings you back to your original starting point.

NORTH VANCOUVER

30 MYSTERY LAKE

Round trip 6.4 km (4 mi)
Allow 2.5 hours
High point 1250 m (4000 ft)
Elevation gain 218 m (700 ft)
Park trails
Best late June to October

What mystery gave this interesting body of water its name we are not now likely to find out. At all events, the lake does provide a pleasant stopover point on what may be a circular hike or a straight there-and-back outing starting from the upper parking lot in Mount Seymour Provincial Park.

From the lower terminal of the Mystery Peak chairlift take the marked trail right across the little basin beneath the right-of-way. Now you start rising among trees, soon losing sight of the pylons and, indeed, of all human activity. After twenty minutes or so of walking, you pass tiny Nancy Lake, with a rocky outcrop above it to the south. A brief detour to this viewpoint rewards you with views of Vancouver and the Fraser lowlands. On resuming, take the trail round the west side of the lake, following it north along a

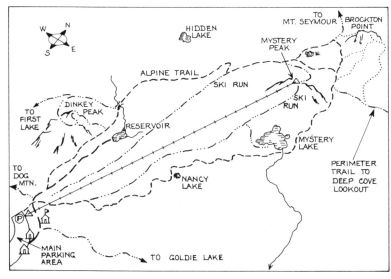

Near the outlet

nice ledge with small cliffs on your left and forest elsewhere. As you advance, the trees gradually thin out and the surroundings become subalpine as you near your objective in its rocky basin.

Here is a spot for rest and contemplation, even if intrusion of the chairlift does spoil the setting to the west. Otherwise, all is natural and it is pleasant to sit on clean rock and let the peace wash over you. Now, however, comes the moment of decision: to return by the trail you have just traversed, a total distance of 3.6 km (2.2 mi) for the trip; or, if you are energetic and adventurous, to continue round the back of Mystery Peak to reach the main Mount Seymour Trail.

To do this, follow the track north over the rocky outcrops on the east side of the lake, then gradually work your way left into the basin between the peak and the imposing rock wall below Brockton Point. In so doing, you see first of all the downhill ski run from the chair's upper terminal, then the hiking trail itself. You turn left on the trail for your return trip.

Nor do you need to tramp down the ski run, barren as it is of shade and vegetation. If you look carefully to its right just as it starts to descend, you will see high on a tree the sign "Alpine Trail" and below it the original and well-used footpath, which takes you down a little valley. On the way down the hiking route, you pass the two ends of Dinkey Peak Loop Trail, an interesting little outing in its own right, and thereafter you soon find yourself dropping back to your point of departure.

31 OLD DOLLAR MILL (Cates Park)

Round trip 2.1 km (1.3 mi)
Allow 1 hour
Beach and park trails
Good all year

This hike may be short on distance; on the other hand, it is long on points of interest that include a cedar grove, Indian relics, and the foundations of the old mill. Add to these a beach walk, a swimming area, and an abundance of harbour and mountain views and you have an outing with enough variety to give an hour's enjoyment, or a day's.

To reach the beginning of this walk, travel east along Dollarton Highway to a point 4.8 km (3 mi) from the Second Narrows Bridge exit. Here, on the right, a sign announces Cates Park. Turn towards the park and drive downhill, looking for a parking spot as far to the west as possible without getting mixed up with the boat-launching traffic. Note also that dogs are not allowed in the park between May 1 and October 1, an indication of how busy the area is in summer, especially on weekends. Unless a swim is on your agenda, therefore, this hike may be saved for off-season when peace reigns and the beauty of the park can be savoured in solitude.

Standing at the wooden jetty by the launching ramp and looking west, you see the buildings of the Matsumoto Shipyard a little way off, with a relic of the seas, the *Island Prince*, tied up at a pier, its days of service long past. Across the harbour stands Burnaby Mountain, its sides disfigured by the paraphernalia of oil refiners but pleasant enough otherwise. From the jetty, which is your departure point, you set off eastwards along the beach, the footing consisting mainly of clean grit, though here and there rounded boulders have to be negotiated with some care.

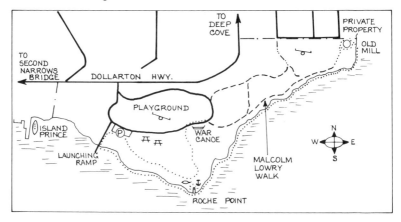

Remains of the mill's furnace room

At Roche Point, identified by its beacon, the waters of Indian Arm join with those of Burrard Inlet and now your route swings north, giving views across to Belcarra Park and to Buntzen Ridge, while Eagle Mountain looms behind to the northeast. But here, too, there is a closer point of interest. On the grassy stretch just above the beach a metal figure of a dolphin appears to frolic a few feet above its natural element. And there is a change in the character of the coastline: little bays alternating with small headlands, the first of these being set aside for swimming while farther along skin divers disport themselves in the clear water.

Finally, at a pile of boulders, a sign announcing a private beach bars further progress along the shore. Scramble here over the rocks to the bank above, where swings and a jungle gym announce a children's playground. And just a little to one side is a low concrete structure much overgrown with moss, all that now remains of the sawmill furnace room, a memorial of sorts to the Scots-Canadian founder of an American shipping line and developer of the mill towards the end of World War I. Round the installation grew the company town of Dollarton, which remained till the mill closed at the end of World War II. From that time on the settlement has been residential though its most famous inhabitant, the novelist Malcolm Lowry, left it with bitter memories, having been evicted to provide space for this very park in which you stand.

The return is among tall trees on a track running parallel with the beach. Eventually this path leads into the open by an Indian totem pole (soon to be followed by another), close to a fifty-foot Indian war canoe. This treasure was created in 1921 by Chief Henry Peter George after a year of loving labour and was donated to the district by his widow. It is a more attractive memento than the mill foundation, and commemorates an older culture. From here the back view of the friendly dolphin is visible beside Roche Point, giving warning that your little trip is almost over.

View from Panorama Park

NORTH VANCOUVER

32 BADEN-POWELL TRAIL (Deep Cove)

Round trip 5.6 km (3.5 mi)
Allow 2 hours
High point 145 m (475 ft)
Forest trail
Good most of the year

It is not often that the destination of a hike is visible or nearly so, from its start, but that is the case here, with a power line pylon on a headland above Indian Arm standing out over the trees that lie between Deep Cove and the objective. In fact, the view from the parking lot at Panorama Park indicates what is to come in its glimpses of small craft on the water and treed bluffs, to the sides of which cling houses in a variety of architectural styles.

Panorama Park is actually a little south of the trail's start, parking on Panorama Drive's 2500 block being very limited. In any case, the view from the park makes a stop here worthwhile, stretching as it does along the shore of a picturesque little bay. Reaching it is not difficult either, the most direct approach being over the Mount Seymour Parkway, carrying straight on at the point where the park highway goes off to the left, descending the hill, then turning left at the stop sign where Dollarton Highway intersects the road. From here, head along Deep Cove Road, veer right onto Gallant Avenue, then swing left on Panorama Drive, and your parking is just off the blacktop on the right.

From the parking lot, descend to the little path that heads north across the grass, passing a picnic site and rejoining the road just at the spot where a large sign announces the existence of the trail, and the further information that this is its eastern terminus. The trail itself heads uphill between houses on the left of the road. Indeed, this first stretch is a good lung-opener as it leads inland and uphill among the trees of an old second-growth forest before turning right once it has made enough height.

Along its route, the path crosses a number of creeks, descending into their ravines then re-emerging on the other side after a crossing by means of Scout-made footbridges. Note also on your left after about 1.6 km (1 mi) the markings for a trail under construction by North Vancouver Parks Board that, when completed, will enable you to turn the latter part of this walk into a circular trip. There is as well a new lookout at 3 km (1.9 mi) on an open bluff to the right with superb views over Indian Arm and back to your starting point.

You may, of course, return from here or from the pylon bluff a short distance beyond, reached via an old dirt road on to which the trail debouches. It is possible, however, to continue on the Baden-Powell trail into the bush on the opposite side of the power line clearing and head up to Indian River Drive, turning left along it to the top of a rise where the Boy Scout trail goes off right. Just beyond this point, on the left, is the other end of the new circuit route.

Descend on this to the original trail and turn right for your return to Deep Cove.

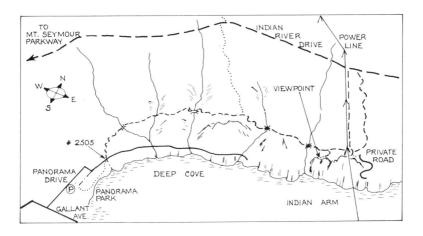

Boat mooring near Steveston

SOUTH OF VANCOUVER

33 LULU ISLAND DYKES

**Round trip (total distance)
21 km (13 mi)
Allow 5.5 hours
Dykes
Good all year**

Here is one of those accommodating outings that provide you with the possibility of one very long walk or two (or more) shorter ones. You may even decide, if time or inclination permits only a brief excursion, whether you want river scenes or views over Sturgeon Bank to the Strait of Georgia.

Travelling south from Vancouver on Highway 99, turn right at the airport exit from Oak Street Bridge, continue on Sea Island Way to the second group of traffic lights, and go left there on No. 3 Road. After some 800 m, turn right on Cambie Road and drive the short distance to its intersection with River Road. Turn left on the latter and park for the long walk; if, however, you wish to split your outing in two, drive along River Road to its western end by the Richmond Riding Club stables.

For the walk downstream, climb to the dyke top for your first view of the river and all its activity. As you travel west, you pass a marina, then a small building, which, from the naval gun mounted beside it, seems to belong to the volunteer armed services. Next you march under Dinsmore Bridge, then come to a beach, Dover Bar, followed by a stretch of free-growing broom, its varied shades an attractive sight in spring. Waterfowl, too, are prominent— herons, Canada geese, even cormorants—while over on Sea Island, aircraft make the distant sky noisy with their arrivals and departures.

So you continue past Swishwash Island to the river mouth and part two of your odyssey. You may feel, however, that a round trip of 10 km (6.2 mi) is sufficient for one day, and save the Steveston section for another occasion. For it, begin where the road ends, working left as the dyke changes direction to the south, becoming wider after you have passed a flood control station at the end of Westminster Highway. You are likely to be less interested, however, in the landward side than in the views across the salt marshes to the Sturgeon Bank where there is an abundance of birdlife.

Towards the south end of your trek, you come on a cluster of radio towers, linked by walkways that march on stiltlike legs across the marshland. Next comes a lagoon, home to a number of fishing craft, beyond which a rough track runs seawards, ending where it joins the river's South Arm. From here you can go no farther by land, so you must retrace your steps, perhaps pondering the chance that led to the immortalizing of Miss Lulu Scott, a young nineteenth-century actress whose performance for the Royal Engineers was thus rewarded.

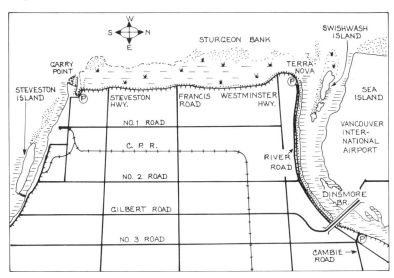

SOUTH OF VANCOUVER

34 RICHMOND NATURE PARK

Round trip 3.2 km (2 mi)
Allow 1.5 hours
Improved trails
Good all year

Motorists speeding south from Vancouver on Highway 99 are very likely unaware of the outdoor pleasure available to them only a few yards from the turnoff to No. 5 Road in Richmond. Here, fronting Westminster Highway, is Richmond Nature Park, the creation of a devoted group of conservationists.

To find this hidden treasure, leave the Deas Island Throughway at the aforementioned turnoff, some 3.2 km (2 mi) south of Oak Street Bridge, and turn right on Westminster Highway. A very short distance along this road on the right is the parking lot for the reserve, next to the park headquarters. In the office, various useful guides are available; so are bags of seed for the inhabitants of the waterfowl pond just a little way inside the gate. There is a picnic area for humans, too, if you wish to make a leisurely round and need sustenance afterwards.

Though the park covers only 108 acres, it is so skillfully laid out that a complete round of the inner and outer circuits comes to just over 3 km (1.9 mi), only a small stretch having to be covered twice. One way to cover the ground effectively is to turn left just inside the park, crossing the end of the bird pond to pay your respects to the pair of swans and the resident geese. The mallard ducks, too, demand attention, if you are providing handouts, and so do the rabbits. Next work your way west along the southern boundary of the park past a stand of small birch, then into a more open area with a variety of shrubs and and bushes, Labrador tea being prominent, especially when it flowers in June. Salal is also found and it flowers about the same time, with the berries ripe by mid-August.

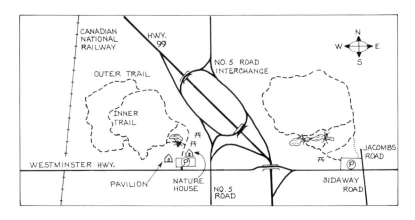

The swans Tony and Cleo

Where the outer ring meets the inner on the north side of the park, small pine trees exist in numbers. Though these are called shore pine in the guide, they have as alternative names scrub or screw pine, perhaps because of their crooked twisted trunks and stunted forms. Unlike many conifers, these trees do not thrive in shade and are usually among the first plants to re-establish themselves after fire; in fact, the heat of fire helps to open the cones and release the seed.

Armed with the park guide you may spend much time identifying these and other plants and one result of your hike may be an enrichment of knowledge. But suppose you are still eager for exercise by the time you have covered the whole area. All you need do is drive east on Westminster Highway, cross the overpass above Highway 99, then turn left at Jacombs Road. Here in a tract corresponding to the one you have just left is Richmond Nature Study Centre with its own small pond and circular trail. To sample its offering, go left into the parking area and start off clockwise past the picnic area to the slough, which you cross on a bridge, then round the park in a wide loop that makes a walk of some 2 km (1.3 mi).

Apart from trail improvements, provision of a picnic shelter, and bridges, little has been done to modify the natural marsh ecology of this part of the peat bog that must have covered much of what is now Richmond townsite and stands as a reminder of the not too distant past.

View downstream across Deas Slough

SOUTH OF VANCOUVER

35 DEAS ISLAND

Round trip 4.4 km (2.7 mi)
Allow 1.5 hours
Park trail
Good all year

Though this is an island only in name, a causeway now connecting the recently created regional park with the mainland south of the Fraser, it still has sufficient water round it to maintain the illusion of its former status. Another interesting feature is that on your walk westwards you cross the southern entrance to the George Massey Tunnel, giving you a view of Highway 99 from above, the route on which you travel south from Vancouver to undertake this outing, which is especially rewarding in winter when the trees are bare and river views are at their best.

Turn off the highway at the Victoria Ferry exit, follow the River Road sign back left across the overpass, but thereafter, at 60th Avenue, go straight ahead on 62B Street. Turn left off this street a little before a sand and gravel operation and enter the park, leaving your vehicle in the first designated parking area. Here you look left to restored heritage buildings, one of which is the park office, and close to the north fork trail (the suggested route) are a commemorative tablet and a lookout tower, the latter providing fine views of the river's main channel below Gravesend Reach.

As you proceed, you pass another parking area on your left, and here you may see the plaque—mounted on an old piston-drive air compressor—that commemorates the park opening. Continuing once more, you arrive at a fork, the left arm of which takes you back by Deas Slough to your point of departure. By staying with the right fork, however, you veer closer to the river's main channel, and, as you cross the tunnel access, you pass the cairn that commemorates its opening in 1959 by Queen Elizabeth II. Your trail west is now a pleasantly rudimentary one as you make for the island's tip, passing an attractive little beach en route.

From there, you look south across the mouth of Deas Slough with its marina lying just to the east of Ladner Marsh. Southwest lies Kirkland Island, a navigation beacon marking its shoal waters. North, of course, is the river, and Lulu Island beyond, the shoreline marked by commercial and industrial operations—freight terminals and the like—though the B.C. Ferries refitting dock does add a touch of maritime romance to the scene.

On your return walk back across the tunnel, you want to go right on the south arm of the loop trail to complete your circular tour of the park. At first you have an interesting sample of marsh ecology as the dyke takes you past wetlands, the trees eye-catching because of the number of nests they carry. Next, you have views south across the waterway that is Deas Slough. At the second viewpoint, stay right on Dyke Loop Trail as another trail forks left. By so doing, you eventually find yourself back where you began your "island" ramble.

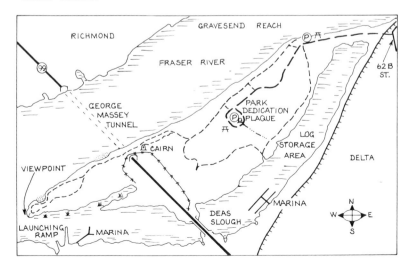

Snow geese

SOUTH OF VANCOUVER

36 REIFEL WILDFOWL REFUGE

Round trip 5 km (3.1 mi)
Allow 2.5 hours
Dyke paths
Good all year, best at migration times

The only possible deterrents to this outing are the admission charges and the limited hours of operation. (For information, call 946-6980.) But if you contrast the tranquillity and the unspoiled surroundings of this estuarine marshland with the tidewater slums of Richmond, that is a small price to pay, taking into account that the B.C. Waterfowl Society, which administers the site, is constantly expanding and improving the facilities. Although tours may be arranged, it is just as much fun to purchase the little booklet that identifies the creatures of the area and make the walk into a self-guided nature tour. You can pick out the different species of birds, notably waterfowl, though shorebirds are not lacking either.

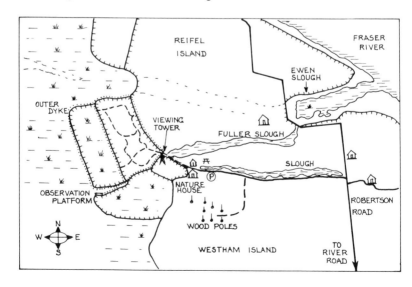

Feeding the Canada geese

Reifel Island itself lies west of Ladner settlement in the municipality of Delta at the mouth of the Fraser River's main channel, where it widens out into a delta; relatively dry land and sandbars alternate with various channels that rejoice in a variety of names: pass, reach, or slough. Actually, the sanctuary is located on part of the larger Westham Island and has access from the mainland by way of a single-lane bridge leading off River Road West. To reach here from Vancouver, take the Victoria Ferry (Highway 17) turnoff from Highway 99 a little south of the George Massey Tunnel, and go south just over 1.6 km (1 mi) to the intersection with 48th Avenue (Ladner Trunk Road). Turn sharp right at the traffic light here and continue west till the road becomes Westham Street, at which point go left one block, then right, to join River Road West. Continue west along this road to the sharp right turn for Westham Island, a distance of 5.6 km (3.5 mi) from the traffic light. Once over the single-lane bridge, the road crosses the farmland of the island, making right-angled turns at the boundaries of fields. Finally, after you have driven alongside a slough noisy with ducks and geese, a small grove with picnic tables appears, and just beyond is the car park. Straight ahead from here is the entrance to the sanctuary leading through the small park office where guidebooks are available. There are also packets of seed to offer the cheerful panhandlers among the resident population or the seasonal visitors.

Though there is a choice of routes in the sanctuary, the one described here covers the whole area as exhaustively as possible, taking into account the possibility that a few areas will have "No Entry" signs at certain times of the year to avoid disturbing such seasonal visitors as the snow geese. First,

View over the entrance to the Refuge

follow the eastern boundary north along the treed dyke with its mixture of shore pine, Douglas-fir, alder, and blackberry bushes. Note the birds in the water of the marsh, or, in winter, round the feeders: Canada geese, snow geese, various ducks, and of course those convivial creatures, the coots, with their uncanny ability to walk on water.

Turning west along the northern boundary, you look out towards Pelly Point— not the most distinguished of landmarks—then marshland fronting Roberts Bank, its treeless dyke and tidal flats supporting varied plant life, of which cattails and tall grasses are the most striking as these rise 180 cm (6 feet) or more among the muddy channels. This track leads back south, giving fine views on a clear day across the strait to the Gulf Islands. Closer at hand, you may see some of the more elusive visitors to the sanctuary, such as trumpeter swans and great blue herons, the latter standing 120 cm (4 feet) tall and looking in the distance like round-shouldered old parsons.

Before beginning the inner circuit, there may be time to visit the open

platform that serves as observation tower for the outer marsh, approached by a narrow causeway and giving a fine panorama over the whole tidal area.

Back on the main dyke, go north outside the wire fence to the gate in the northwest corner. Enter by this gate and travel south on the bank that follows a sinuous course through the marsh, enjoying the sight of all the varied winged guests as they pursue their proper activities. Note what a noisy place the sanctuary is: there are geese honking, ducks quacking, wings beating when a group rises from the water, and the continual chattering of the varied species.

This part of the trip makes a very irregular Z, quartering the marsh and ending near the main observation tower. From here, the whole area is spread out from the entrance road in the south to the houses of Steveston across the river to the north, and the Reifel farm across to the east. Below, too, is the Nature House offering interpretive displays, which you may want to visit if you did not do so on your arrival at the sanctuary.

Great blue heron – B.C. Dept. of Recreation and Conservation

SOUTH OF VANCOUVER

37 BRUNSWICK POINT

Round trip 10.4 km (6.5 mi)
Allow 3 hours
Dyke
Good all year

Whether you start or end your walk at the point is a matter of preference; certainly the site of a one-time cannery fronting on Canoe Pass and the estuarine flats of the Fraser is a more scenic destination than the causeway leading to Roberts Bank Coal Terminal, but even the latter is not without a certain stark attractiveness—seen from a distance.

To reach the north end, leave Highway 99 as if heading for the Reifel wildlife refuge (see Walk 36). This time, however, stay on River Road West to its end. This spot in itself is a nice one for lazing as you look from its jetty across the river mouth to Westham Island or over the strait to the Vancouver Island mountains. As you walk south, check the marsh for birdlife; in addition to a wide variety of shorebirds, including grebes and bitterns, you may see an occasional hawk, probably because the seaward-side marsh is here balanced by arable land beyond the drainage ditch. Finally, comes the landward end of the coal-port causeway, a possible turning point. You may, however, go a little farther southeast before you come to the Tsawwassen Indian Reserve, necessitating an about-turn.

If you are using the south end as your point of departure, you should turn left off River Road West on 41B Street and drive to Matheson Road, on which you turn right to reach the dyke close by the Roberts Bank railway crossing. Park by the dyke gate and, depending on your inclination, either travel northwest towards the cannery or southeast on the short stretch to the margin of Indian land.

Yet one more possibility exists if you wish to include the lower stretch of the Fraser's South Arm in your itinerary. For this, park where the gated dyke begins a little west of Morris Road, mount the ramp to the top of the embankment and proceed westwards to the sea, eventually reaching the one-time cannery site from the east and adding about 600 m to your total distance.

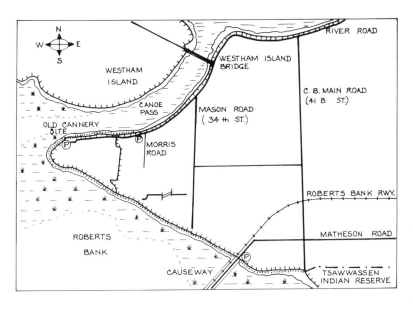

Gull prints

SOUTH OF VANCOUVER

38 BOUNDARY BAY

Round trip (northern section)
8 km (5 mi)
Allow 3 hours
Round trip (southern section)
6.4 km (4 mi)
Allow 2 hours
Dyke and beach
Good all year

Since the total dyke length from Mud Bay in the east to Beach Grove at its western end is 16 km (10 mi), only the super-fit, cyclists, and two-car groups are likely to attempt it in its entirety. Fortunately, there are numerous intermediate access points, so, by selecting one of them, you may choose the distance you wish to cover in this highly interesting area, with its marine and mountain views and variety of birdlife.

From Highway 99 a short distance south of the George Massey Tunnel, go right on Highway 17 and follow it for 2.3 km (1.4 mi) to its intersection with Highway 10 (Ladner Trunk Road). Turn left here and, as you drive eastwards, the various beach access roads are on your right. The first, 64th Street, provides a short walk to the southwest before the dyke ends at Beach Grove, necessitating a trek along a rather oozy stretch if you wish to continue. The next, 72nd Street, gives you a nice round trip west and south-

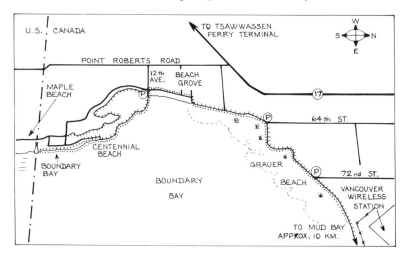

View south from Maple Beach

west covering nearly 8 km (5 mi), just the thing to bring colour to your cheeks on a cool winter day.

The whole area is particularly rich in birdlife. Ducks, of course, are common, but you may come across a snowy owl if you are lucky, and hawks and bald eagles may also be seen on the stretch between the dyke and the sands of the bay. A special feature in April is the spring stopover of black brant on their migration northwards from their winter habitat along the U.S. west coast. If you start travelling westwards, your view is towards the promontory of Point Roberts, with the San Juan Islands looming romantically in the background. The return journey gives you, by contrast, the mountains of Vancouver's North Shore, stretching east to Golden Ears Mountain, with Mount Baker dominant to the southeast.

Between the end of 72nd Street and the next approach east, 88th Street, lies the presently inactive Boundary Bay Airport, the future of which has been under discussion for some time past, one suggestion being its reactivation as a landing field for small planes, a not too pleasant prospect. There is less variety on this stretch of dyke; indeed, the farther east you go, the more uniform becomes the landscape. Thus, though 96th, 104th, and 112th streets all provide access to, and experience of, the north end of Mud Bay, the more rewarding walks start at the other points mentioned.

Should you wish to confine your outing to only the southwest section of the bay, continue south on Highway 17 as far as 56th Street (Point Roberts Road), on which you go left. At 12th Avenue (Boundary Bay Road), go left again and drive east to the road end by the Centennial Park Beach sign, a little south of the oozy section of coast mentioned earlier. The track first takes you east; soon, however, it veers south and disappears among the coarse grass behind the beach proper. Now you are looking along the shore to the international boundary and Point Roberts as you continue on the sand.

At the park's south end are the houses of the little settlement of Boundary Bay, stretching almost to the beach but still leaving room for walking if you would like to go as far as the 49th parallel before retracing your steps through this park, which is administered by the Greater Vancouver Regional District.

Pair of Canada geese

SOUTH OF VANCOUVER

39 SERPENTINE FEN

Round trip 4.5 km (2.8 mi)
Allow 1.5 hours
Dykes
Good all year

For some years Delta has been able to boast of its wildlife refuge on Reifel Island; now Surrey can match its neighbour with this wildfowl sanctuary located just south of the Serpentine River and between Highway 99 and King George Highway, access being from the latter.

If you are coming south from the city on 99, go off it at the King George Interchange, cross the overpass, and drive north the short distance to Wade Road; turn westwards here just beyond the garden shop and drive past the gate (open 9:00 A.M. to 5:00 P.M. every day) to the parking lot on your left. Here your circuit begins as you continue west to the observation tower, a climb to the top of which gives you a bird's-eye view of the reserve and across the river to the higher ground on its north bank.

Resuming your clockwise walk, you carry on almost to the freeway before turning first northwest, then north towards the river. On this stretch, too, the Environment Ministry is constructing an observation tower, providing you with the opportunity for a second ascent, this one having major views east and west. Next comes the river itself, its numerous twists and turns testifying to the appropriateness of its name, and along it you head eastwards, then south, conforming to its sinuous course.

As you once more resume your easterly direction, you come to a fork and at this point you follow the route to the right, which takes you back towards the original tower and the completion of your circular walk.

Actually, the left-hand trail at the fork just mentioned does give another approach from immediately south of the King George Highway bridge over the Serpentine; thus you may make the loop in counterclockwise direction after parking just off the road and walking downstream along the river dyke to the parting of the ways.

Note that public access to this interesting area is limited to the outer circle, the central section being reserved strictly for the birds, an interesting and varied assortment that includes mallards, Canada geese, widgeon, and red-tailed hawks. These, of course, make up the resident population, but in fall and spring their numbers are greatly augmented by migrants proceeding south or north according to the season. Less welcome are the muskrats, those busy tunnellers of the animal kingdom whose activities tend to undermine the dykes that keep the river within bounds.

It remains only to mention involvement in this project by the wildlife branch of the Environment Ministry, aided by voluntary efforts of local naturalist groups. Their reward? Greater public interest in this province's rich natural history.

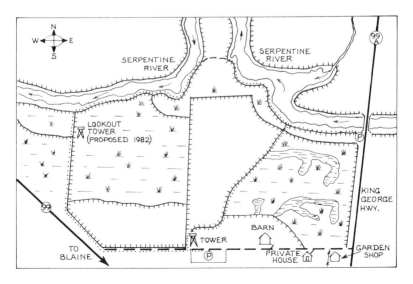

40 CRESCENT BEACH

Round trip 8.4 km (5.2 mi)
Allow 3 hours
Beach and roads
Good all year

This stretch of coastline lying along the east side of Boundary Bay lends itself to a number of outings: a short one north to Blackie Spit or Mud Bay—more attractive than its name suggests—and several longer excursions south towards Ocean Park, including White Rock and Semiahmoo Bay as possibilities if you wish a really lengthy beach walk.

Coming south on Highway 99, leave it at the King George Highway Interchange and follow Crescent Road westwards, crossing the railway tracks onto Beech Street. Then, to avoid parking problems on weekends and to give yourself a longer walk, fork right on Sullivan and go right again on McBride to its end in a parking area by some tennis courts, a little south of Blackie Spit. This land projects northeastwards into the bay with its tidal marshes that support much wildlife, including a number of seals, which may be seen disporting themselves on the mudbanks.

For the beach walk southwards, you begin in the park area following a route that takes you round a small point, then in front of a row of attractive cottages, with, finally, a waterfront of pebbles or shingle and the Burlington Northern tracks between you and the cliff. After some forty minutes on foot, note the stairway descending the cliff, the return route if you wish to make this a loop walk. As you wander southwards, you may enjoy the trees of the steep scarp slope on your left when you are not taking in the marine view

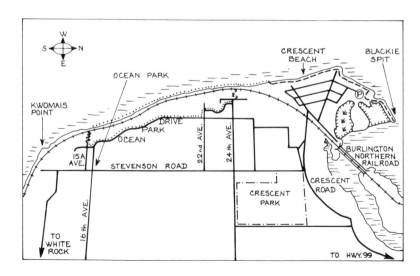

Crescent Beach

with islands and points of land rising from the waters. At last, after another thirty-five minutes, you come to a pedestrian underpass of the railway, with a cliff stairway behind, and here you should ascend if you wish to leave the beach for a time and take in some of the residential areas of Ocean Park.

On top of the bluffs at 15A Avenue follow Ocean Park Drive north until on 22nd Avenue you go left for one block then continue right on Harbour Greene Drive to 24th Avenue, a distance of 2.2 km (1.4 mi) on reasonably quiet roads. On 24th turn left and at its end descend once more to the beach for your return northwards, this time with Bowen Island and the mountains of Vancouver's North Shore before your eyes.

SOUTH OF VANCOUVER

41 REDWOOD PARK

Round trip 2 km (1.2 mi)
Allow 1.5 hours
Forest trails and lawns
Good all year

Don't be put off by the small area of this park—only twenty-six hectares (sixty-four acres). Because of its unique and attractive collection of trees bordering on shady lawns, you may easily follow its varied trails for a good hour or more.

Redwood Park more than lives up to its name. Its original owners—eccentric twin brothers, Peter and David Brown—made a hobby of collecting the seeds of various trees and planting them in this property. Among these are redwoods from California and, though there are such South American exotics as monkey puzzles in one of the groves, there are also more everyday conifers such as cedar, pine, and fir. In fact, part of the charm of the place is the memory of the pioneer Surrey family that lived here, finally ending up in a large tree house that is still to be seen in a dense clump of timber.

The park is somewhat isolated considering that it is only 48 km (30 mi) southeast of Vancouver. Probably the easiest approach from Highway 99 is to go south from it on King George Highway as far as North Bluff Road (16th Avenue) on the outskirts of White Rock. Turn left (east) on this road to 178th Street (Highway 15), go left (north) for about 800 m to 20th Avenue, where you turn right and continue till you see the parking lot signs near the park's east side, facing the main area with its tables.

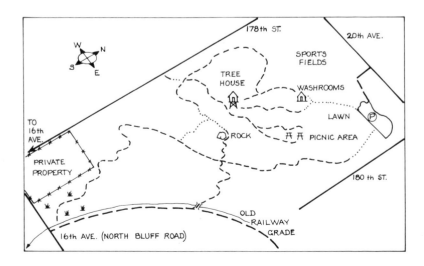

The tree house

From here, head a little northwest to pick up a main trail (by the washroom) that leads you into the forest. You have a sense of the different trees in the park and identification of them keeps you guessing. By turning a little south you come out on one of the open grassy areas with trees on all sides except to the southwest, where you look out to the U.S. border and the San Juan Islands. Close to one of these clearings, too, is the tree house with a short account of its building and function on a wooden signboard beside it.

Though you may put in your time here in simply wandering the park trails at random, the following circular outing covers most of its features, once you have viewed the tree dwelling. From it follow the trail west then swing back along the lower edge of the clearing to pick up a trail heading downhill from its southeast corner by a large boulder, perhaps a glacial erratic. Next go right on a path marked by red diamonds curving back left along the edge of some private property to an old railway grade a little north of North Bluff Road.

Follow this grade as it rises northeastwards, then, after some ten minutes, go left over a bridge on a trail back up into the park. From it, turn right at a T-junction and continue uphill to emerge on the lawn a little south of the picnic tables and the parking area.

View over Campbell Valley

SOUTH OF VANCOUVER

42 CAMPBELL VALLEY PARK

Round trip 13.2 km (8.2 mi)
Allow 4 hours
Park trails
Good all year

The stream that flows through the centre of this recreation area rises at the south end of Langley Municipality and pursues its course gently westwards, running roughly parallel with the Canada–U.S. border except for one hairpinlike swing to the north followed by return to its original direction. Thereafter it ends uneventfully in Semiahmoo Bay, just south of White Rock.

On its northwards jog, it is crossed by 16th Avenue (North Bluff Road). This you reach by leaving Highway 99 at the King George Highway turnoff and driving south on the latter for about 6.4 km (4 mi) before turning left. After you have crossed the intersection with 200th Street, 16th descends into the valley and, on your right, you see an entrance that leads to a parking area. Now, you have a variety of choices, ranging from a short walk on the valley floor to a half-day circuit using a trail open to both hiking and horse traffic.

For the former, simply head south from the park indicator board, at first through trees, then across a scenic meadow for some fifteen minutes before going left to cross the stream on a boardwalk. Once across, another left brings you back along the east side of the valley for a pleasant outing lasting about an hour. To begin the longer walk, go back north a little then turn east on the cedar-chip trail, cross the stream, and rise to level ground. Now you have a nice variety of pastoral country as you travel south, noting as you go a foot trail descending to the right, giving another access to the valley floor if you desire to use it.

The hiking/riding trail, after a jog east, resumes its southerly direction, passes an equestrian centre, near which another trail drops off right; you, however, continue, passing Langley Speedway—at present disused—then dropping gently to the valley floor in an area that may be damp after rain. Next comes a turn to the right at a major fork and your crossing of the river, followed by a stretch of open parklike country as you gradually veer south and west, preparatory to turning north, this last stretch being amid attractive woodland.

The actual park centre is reached at 8th Avenue, but before you get to this point, turn right again to some one-time farm buildings. By so doing, you see what is intended to become a "historic farmstead", even including the old machines. Now you turn north again to the picnic area just above the valley, and here you may wish to rest for a little before going a short distance back west to pick up your trail again. Of course, you may take the foot trail into the valley from here but, on a sunny day especially, it is pleasant to stay above, traversing meadows and skirting stretches of woodland, past numerous ponds, the homes of various ducks, especially mallards. Finally, as you come in sight of 16th again, you do drop down to the valley floor, back to your original point of departure.

This walk is attractive at all seasons. In spring and summer the valley is rich in flowers, trillium being a particular feature around Easter time. In fall, the blackberrying is an attraction in itself, and even winter need not deter you, for, with the trees bare, you have vistas that are concealed at other seasons.

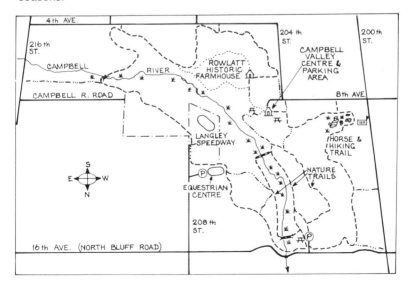

View down Burrard Inlet

EAST OF VANCOUVER

43 CAPITOL HILL

Round trip 4.4 km (2.7 mi)
Allow 1.5 hour
High point 280 m (900 ft)
Elevation gain 120 m (400 ft)
Forest trails and streets
Good all year

Feel like a good lung-opener on a winter day, or some exercise on a summer evening with glorious views as a reward? Harbourview Park on the summit of the hill serves admirably as a destination for this walk, partly on forest paths, partly on quiet residential streets, with a beginning in one park and a destination in another.

To reach the start of your excursion, drive north on Willingdon Avenue five blocks beyond its intersection with East Hastings then turn right on Penzance Drive. Turn right again into the parking lot by the bowling green in

Confederation Park and pause to survey the task ahead—steadily uphill. Still, you do have grass underfoot as you set off eastwards, making for Cambridge Street, which breasts the hill in front of you. Go uphill one block then bear left on Bessborough, which leads to Scenic Drive with its "No Exit" sign, a distance of 600 m.

At this road end, take the trail into the forest but very soon turn right uphill on quite a steep track. This brings you to another turnaround at the north end of Hythe Street. Continue uphill on the grassy easement beyond the last house, but just before the next level, strike off bearing left again on a foot trail, slightly overgrown, for the last stretch of your climb to Harbourview Park. Here, you have views north up Indian Arm and across to the mountains of the North Shore and there are seats if you want to get your breath back before descending. You may, of course, return by the route just described, but for a superb outlook westwards over Vancouver go one block south on Grosvenor or Ranelagh avenues and descend from the top by Cambridge Street, one with no through traffic, being blocked halfway down by a handy power station.

Even when you have returned to the foot of Cambridge Street where it turns right on North Beta Avenue you need not go immediately to your car. Walk north on Beta, cross Penzance Street just west of the Chevron Training Centre, and immediately opposite you find a nature trail taking you into forest above Burrard Inlet. This, too, is furnished with benches and views across the harbour. There are even unofficial trails to the water; these, however, involve crossing the C.P.R. tracks so, naturally, you do not use them. As you work your way westwards, you cross a little creek with a fork just beyond; go left and uphill here and soon you find yourself back at Penzance Street, just opposite the car park, your outing over.

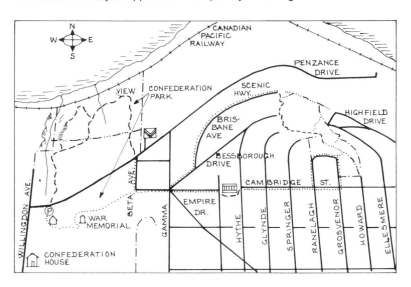

Trillium

EAST OF VANCOUVER

44 BURNABY MOUNTAIN

Round trip 8 km (5 mi)
Allow 3 hours
Trails
Good all year

Everyone knows that Simon Fraser University is situated on top of Burnaby Mountain; not so many are aware, perhaps, that the mountain is also the site of Burnaby's Centennial Park, which lies about 800 m to the west of its illustrious neighbour. It is in the park, though, that this walk has its beginning and end, the two separated by a circle of about 8 km (5 mi).

The easiest way to reach Centennial Park is to drive east on Curtis Street in Burnaby, using Sperling Avenue to get to it by coming north from Trans-Canada Way or the Lougheed Highway, or south from Hastings Street. Curtis starts rising as the houses thin out after you have been on it for a short distance. At the intersection with Gaglardi Way, turn left on Centennial Way and drive to the parking lot by the pavilion, situated on a commanding spur overlooking Burrard Inlet and giving deference only to the proud mountains of the north.

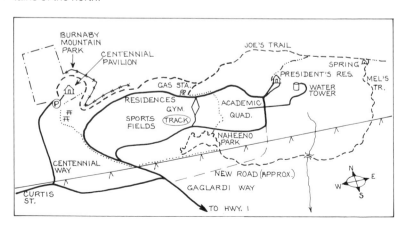

View north up Indian Arm

From here set off uphill past the two presentation totem poles, keeping the wire fence on your left. Pass by the children's playground and emerge finally on a stretch to the left of the one-way road leading from Simon Fraser University. Here a well-defined trail strikes off to the left in the second-growth forest on the north side of the mountain, below the crest and out of sight of the university though linked with it by two trails on the uphill side. This trail travels eastwards, dropping a little as it progresses and is shaded by tall trees. After a little less than 3.2 km (2 mi), at a seat by a small spring, a foot trail—"Mel's"—strikes off uphill to the right.

On this trail you swing round the east side of the mountain, catching occasional glimpses of the works of man below, including the Port Mann Bridge, which carries freeway traffic over the Fraser River. In your progress, the trail intersects a power line; otherwise it meanders along—now up, now down— crossing two or three small creeks on wooden footbridges, which may be slippery when wet. Next comes an old access road, followed by a newly constructed highway that you must also cross, using the red markers as guides. And then you reach the power line once more.

This is your point of decision. You may follow the power line westwards downhill till it reaches Gaglardi Way just below its fork. From here you must go half right and uphill on the grass verge for some 400 m, then go left and back into Centennial Park by its picnic tables. This route, however, can be wet and messy so it is probably more rewarding to stay right, enter the forest on its north side, and, by partial circuit of Naheeno Park, come out at Arthur Erickson's architectural creation, Simon Fraser University. Cross the campus by any route you fancy, finally arriving at the west end of the academic area where, just by the gas station and bus stop on the north side of the ring road, you may drop down to your original route for the return.

Park entrance

EAST OF VANCOUVER

45 BURNABY BIG BEND

Round trip 3.6 km (2.2 mi)
Allow 1 hour
Park trail
Good all year

This walk along an attractive stretch of the river is south of S.E. Marine Drive in Burnaby's Big Bend district, an area once devoted to market gardens but now, alas, falling victim to industrial development. To reach your starting point turn sharp south off Marine Drive on Byrne Road, located some distance east of Boundary Road. Follow this towards the river then turn left on Fraser River Drive to park as closely as you can at the road's eastern end in Burnaby Fraser Foreshore Park. (Note: Construction, when completed, of Marine Way, parallel with and south of Marine Drive, will make it the preferred approach.)

Since your main walk is downstream, head for the river walkway, flanked by picnic tables and benches on your right hand. Now you enjoy the varied vistas afforded by the bend of the stream, its trees lining either bank giving it something of the appearance of the lower Rhine, but your route is quite soon interrupted by a slough; all you need do, however, is walk a few paces north to a gate with a trail beyond it and continue through a balsam grove, the scent of which perfumes the spring air. Less appealing to the olfactory organ is the odour of skunk cabbage, however pleasing that plant may be to the eye with its bold yellow flowers.

So you proceed westwards, noting the fussy tugs and other river traffic and revelling in the bird song that fills the grove. Away to the northwest, too, are the Lions, looking remote and forbidding from this distance. En route, you cross yet another slough, and now you have trees to the left and right of you as you leave the bank for a time, returning to it only at your walk's destination—a pipeline, of all unromantic things. You may, of course, continue if you wish but you soon find yourself confronted by a sawmill, so it is probably best to retrace your steps from the last river viewpoint.

As you head back upstream, you become conscious of motor traffic on River Road, which runs along the south bank, mercifully screened from view for a fair part of the time by trees so that the effect, in the main, is rural. As you come back to the developed section of the park, you note an attractive little beach, a popular playground for youngsters, even if swimming is discouraged as being too dangerous.

Incidentally, if you like exploring, you may go eastwards from the upstream end of the park via an easement through an industrial plant and continue upriver on an overgrown old road as far as the C.N.R. embankment and trans-river bridge. Beyond this point, though, the route deteriorates and finally disappears in the undergrowth.

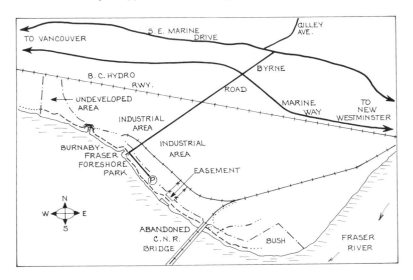

EAST OF VANCOUVER

46 CENTRAL PARK

Round trip 4.3 km (2.7 mi)
Allow 1.5 hours
Forest trails
Good all year

Anyone who has driven along Kingsway between Vancouver and New Westminster knows the north end of this park with its tall trees and sports stadium if only because of the B.C. Hydro Railway's crossing that acts as a deterrent to low-fliers trying to prove that Burnaby's traffic signals are not set for 50 km/h. North-end parking is just east of the stadium and is approached by a road that turns right off Kingsway (for anyone coming from Vancouver) a little beyond the Burnaby Road traffic light. The park entrance is marked by a pair of tall stone pillars, a kind of ceremonial gateway. Once past these, drive a short distance to the parking lot situated between Swangard Stadium and treed lawns with their picnic tables.

From here, various main trails lead deeper into the forest; the route described, though, covers all the chief features of one of the oldest lower mainland recreation areas. To begin with, head away from the stadium to pick up a trail that begins just by the washrooms. This trail takes you off southeastwards though it does wind somewhat in the timber, which, as the silent stumps of once great trees indicate, is second-growth forest. Stay left at the first main intersection but at the second go right as you follow the path that takes you mainly south. Note after some fifteen minutes' walking the construction on the left: an underground reservoir with tennis courts on its roof.

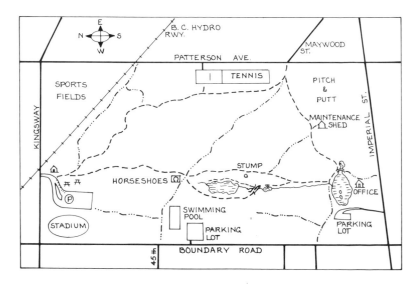

Model boat pond

At this point, close to the park's eastern boundary and Patterson Avenue, another trail joins from the west; just beyond, where Maywood Street unites with Patterson, there is yet one more route bearing off to the right following the split-rail fence of the pitch-and-putt course that occupies the southeast corner. Follow this, pausing from time to time to feast your eyes on the views between the trees of the golf course, over the Fraser Delta, and all the way south to Point Roberts. A short distance along this trail another comes in from the right, but only those in a mad rush to get home need take it; in fact, it cuts off one of the park's most interesting features, the pond where model yachts are sailed, just by the golf course entrance.

Close to this body of water is another parking lot, this one approached from Imperial Street, so that you could reverse your walk if you wish and start it here instead. In any event, it is now that you turn north, using a trail parallelling the small stream that flows through a Japanese-type garden on its way to add its water to the model boating pond. Some fifteen minutes along this route is a larger body of water to the south of the horseshoe pitching ground, located not far from the 45th Avenue entrance. From this point, the forest path runs directly back to the stadium and your car.

Obviously, on a walk like this a number of variations are possible. The section in the southeast corner may be lengthened, for instance, by following the outside fence of the golf course along Patterson to Imperial, then going west along that street towards the boating pond. The only drawback to this plan is the traffic on your left.

Burnaby Art Gallery

EAST OF VANCOUVER

47 DEER LAKE (Century Park)

Round trip 4 km (2.5 mi)
Allow 1.5 hours
Park trails
Good all year

Apart from this park in Burnaby, there are probably few locations in the Lower Mainland where you may, from one parking spot, visit an art gallery, explore a re-created village, stroll through formal gardens, and enjoy a walk along the recently extended trail system west and south of Deer Lake. Here the city's art collection is housed in a one-time mansion, its carefully preserved gardens providing a fitting setting. Downhill to the east, beyond the associated fine arts centre, is Heritage Village (open every day but Monday during the summer; phone 604-291-8525 for details), where you may even treat yourself to a ride on the miniature railway. South of this area lies the lake, a setting for various waterfowl as well as small boats, the latter emanating from Deer Lake Park proper, a separate small recreation site with a beach, reached from Sperling Avenue.

To get to this garden of delights from Vancouver, follow Canada Way east through Burnaby, go right and uphill a little way past the Municipal Hall to Gilpin, and park by the art gallery. From here you may indulge your curiosity, enjoying the gardens, especially in May when their rhododendrons are in flower, or wandering down to the lake with its short walk along the bank lush with irises and roses.

But there is more to Deer Lake than this. Ascend the hill past the children's playground with its homes for elves and gnomes and, having walked to the Gilpin Street entrance, turn left for about 100 m along the roadway. Next, go left again on Rowan Street, followed by a right onto Price. This dead end gives access to a trail that actually comes in from Gilpin but farther down the hill, so make another turn left through a small section of forest before arriving at another trail junction. The one stretching straight ahead westwards gives access from Royal Oak Avenue; you, however, walk left once more, cross a still creek, and follow round the end of the lake, the bulk of the one-time Oakalla Prison brooding over you as you advance amid irises and shrubs such as Labrador tea.

Gradually your trail veers eastwards along the lake's south shore and once again you come to a fork. The route descending the hill from the south gives yet another approach, coming from the junction of Oakland and Dufferin, the former reached from Royal Oak. A walk up this hill gives you good views north to Burnaby Mountain and the North Shore peaks, but you must retrace your steps. Should you go straight along the level trail, you reach a fence with a gate, beyond which a small creek drains into the lake. From here you may walk out to a sandspit, looking across to where you started, and this at present is as far as you can go officially, since private property lies beyond.

The most striking feature of this area is its pleasing pastoral apearance; you can forget briefly that you are in a city as you walk the trails, or indulge in some of the other pastimes available here.

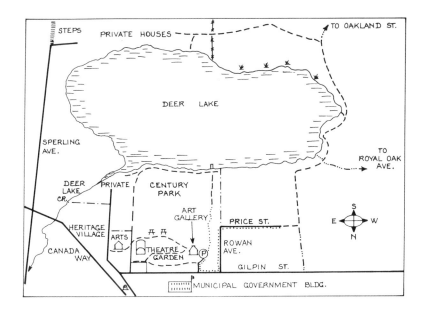

48 ROBERT BURNABY PARK

Round trip 3.2 km (2 mi)
Allow 1.5 hours
Bridle trail and footpath
Good all year

That this little gem of a park is not better known is probably because it does not lie handy to a main thoroughfare. Even though Highway 1 runs at the foot of the park, it does not provide access. So the hurrying vehicles rush past, their drivers unconscious of what they are missing: walks in well laid out ravine trails or forest glades having grassy lawns, and even an open-air swimming pool.

To reach this spot from Vancouver is a trifle complicated, involving as it does a drive along Kingsway past Central Park and through Burnaby for another thirty blocks to Edmonds Street. Go left here, follow Edmonds past its intersection with Canada Way, turn south on 6th Street for two short blocks, swing left on 18th Avenue, and, after two blocks more, left again on 2nd Street. Now the park is straight ahead—but not the parking. For this, you must turn left again at the eastern end of the developed park and, on Hill Avenue, head downhill as far as you can drive to the large parking lot and picnic area just south of Highway 1.

On arrival, look about you. Uphill lies the park; down the wooded slopes in a picturesque ravine flows a small creek crossed here and there by foot-bridges. On the other side of Highway 1 looms Burnaby Mountain with the low-set mass of Simon Fraser University capping its top. Behind are higher

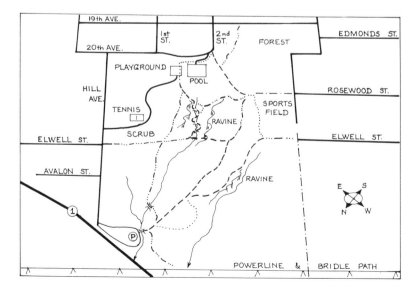

Ravine in Robert Burnaby Park

mountaintops promising wider views once you get out and stretch your legs on the climb.

One route keeps to the west of the creek system, taking you uphill among tall trees with the little stream on your left and below you, and with occasional cross trails coming up to join the main path as it stretches upwards. Finally by keeping right, you arrive on a small sports field at the edge of the park just above a notice warning of a dangerous ravine. Cut left from here towards the trees and soon a way opens through them, one that brings you out to the pretty little open-air swimming pool if you take the right-hand branch at each of two successive forks. Just beyond is the upper car park and beyond that is a children's playground imaginatively laid out among tall trees set well apart. From here, too, the view up the Coquitlam River to the mountain of the same name and the western side of Burke Ridge is truly impressive, particularly when, in spring, snow is gleaming in the sun.

There is still plenty to see, however, as you start wending your way downhill, this time starting on the east side of the creek. Now you look across Burnaby Lake in its shallow trough towards the mountain backdrop, while close at hand is the winding stream. Watch for a path dropping left on some steps into the ravine, then go right down the winding trail till it meets a major intersecting route. Go left here, climb to meet yet another trail and turn right on it, then continue downhill towards the spot where your vehicle is located. Before you leave, however, wander over to the open grassy stretch among the trees to the west; it is a perfect miniature forest glade, especially with the sun streaking through the tall trees and onto the grass, creating patterns of light and shade.

49 BURNABY LAKE

Round trip 12.8 km (8 mi)
Allow 4 hours
Park trails
Good most of the year

Development of the trail system both west and east of the original park nucleus with a crossing of Still Creek giving access to Burnaby Sports Complex supplies you with an exceptional variety of choices of starting points and destinations. There is only one thing the park does lack: a complete lake circuit, some private property at its east end forcing the would-be walker onto roads; the described outings, therefore, involve returning by your original route.

One possible beginning is at the lake's rowing pavilion parking lot. To reach this from Highway 1 travelling east, go off on Sprott Street at the sign for Kensington Avenue (North). Turn left and then, at the traffic lights beyond the overpass, travel straight forward towards Burnaby Sports Complex. At the T-junction, go right on Sperling following signs for the Lake Pavilion, parking for which is reached by a left turn onto Roberts Street. Stop close to the entrance and look for a path, signposted "Central Valley," on the north side of the road.

This takes you by way of some interesting marsh surroundings to a right fork that leads you round playing fields to the footbridge over Still Creek. Note that the sports complex parking lot, which you pass on your left, provides another possible start if you want a walk shorter by 2.4 km (1.5 mi) than this one. In any event, cross the creek and turn right on the nature trail that runs along the north side of the lake—specially interesting in late sum-

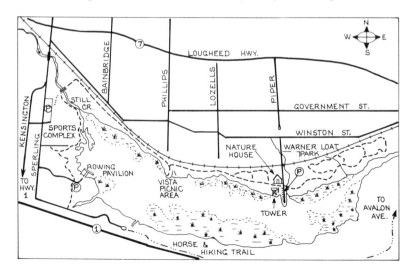

Sign at the Piper Road entrance

mer with water lilies in flower and the masses of purple loosestrife on the marshes surrounding it. Eventually you reach the Bird Watching Tower and the Nature House, the area being a bird sanctuary as well as a park. Having come this far, you may feel that you have gone far enough, your one-way trip to here having been about 4 km (2.5 mi).

There is, however, a whole new trail system to the east of the little jetty, extending in a series of linked circular paths for another 4.8 km (3 mi). If you wish to make a separate trip of this, use the parking area by the Nature House; to reach this point by car, stay left at the sports complex traffic light, go north on Sperling to the Burlington Northern Railroad crossing, and, immediately beyond, turn right on Winston Street. Drive east, then turn right again on Piper Avenue at the park sign.

On this approach, just before your second crossing of the tracks, note attractive little Warner Loat Park with its picnic tables, a pleasant spot to refresh yourself after your exertions.

Brunette River below the weir

EAST OF VANCOUVER

50 BRUNETTE RIVER

Round trip 7 km (4.5 mi)
Allow 2 hours
Dirt road and park path
Good all year

For most people, the only contact with this waterway is a tiny sign at a Highway 1 overpass between the Cariboo Road and Brunette Avenue turn-offs. Well, at least one stretch of the stream is suited for walking, with the route described here having as its destination a small park just inside New Westminster, a possible picnic spot if you wish to combine lunch with your hike.

From Highway 1 eastbound, turn off on Cariboo Road, cross the overpass and stay right for a short distance, then go left on Cariboo North and under the overpass. Cross the river, double back at Love Kennels, and go under the overpass again to a gate on your left just beyond. Alternatively from the Lougheed Highway, turn south on Brighton, go left on Government Street, then right on Cariboo at a railroad crossing.

As you proceed, you have small second-growth alder on the left, with large blackberry bushes sporting vicious looking thorns. Across the stream, on the right, are tall trees, but between you and them are road and river, the latter flowing in sprightly fashion at first, then gradually becoming still and a little sinister looking. The mystery, however, is soon cleared up: two successive weirs hold back the waters and are responsible for the silence. In your progress, you become aware of the railway on the left, screened though it is by trees and bushes; in fact, something of the thrill of railroads comes back if a freight or passenger train passes along.

Eventually, though, another kind of traffic becomes audible as a second gate appears just ahead, beyond which is the busy North Road. This need not be the destination of your hike, however. At the road, turn right, cross the river on the bridge, then enter Hume Park, a recreation area administered by the New Westminster Parks Board. At its entrance a flat grassy field with picnic tables and washrooms stretches ahead until it is enclosed by the old banks of the river, indication that the stream once made quite a bend here. To the right, a sign points to a nature path that contours the hillside, gradually rising to a sports field.

Stroll in this pleasant area heading towards the fenced-off stretch extending almost to the riverbank. At the very edge, however, a trail leads downhill, back to the lower level. From now, you are on your return trip, and once again North Road has to be negotiated. This is not always the simplest of matters, but thereafter you follow the peaceful road along the river. At least it should be peaceful, but occasionally you may be annoyed by motorbikers on it, despite the efforts of Burnaby police to keep them off. The police advice for dealing with motorbikers in places where they do not belong is to report them as soon as you can.

To end on a pleasanter note, did you connect the dark hue of the waters of Brunette River with its name or did you simply assume that the colour was the result of pollution? Well, there may be a little of the latter, but the stream received its colour and thus its name, according to *1001 British Columbia Place Names*, from the peaty ground by its source in Burnaby Lake.

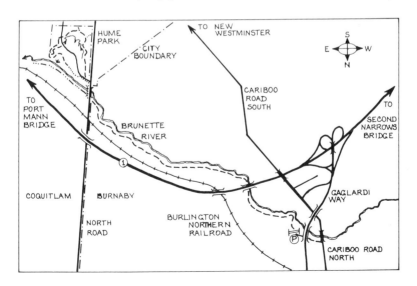

Mundy Lake

EAST OF VANCOUVER

51 MUNDY LAKE PARK

Round trip 5 km (3 mi)
Allow 2 hours
Park trails
Good all year

For a pleasant afternoon outing on well laid out forest trails, with intriguing views of small lakes, try this delightful park located near the eastern boundary of Coquitlam Municipality. The body of water from which the park takes its name is attractive in itself, but so is its less easily discovered neighbour to the east, named, appropriately enough, Lost Lake.

From Highway 1 going east, turn off north at the Cariboo Interchange to join the Lougheed Highway, on which you turn right. Continue east but eventually go left and uphill on Austin Avenue. Stay on Austin for some 4.5 km (2.8 mi) then go left on Hillcrest Street—and suddenly you are at your destination, the park's south parking area. Here you are close to sports fields with washrooms just north of you, beyond which is yet another parking space, an access road leading into it.

Walk to this lot, taking the track along its east side, then passing the small ornamental lakes and swimming pool. Next comes the senior sports field followed by the intersection with a main gravel track; ignore this track and continue north behind Hillcrest School to where your route goes off sharp right at a T-junction (continuing north here brings you to Como Lake Avenue). Go east on this new trail, crossing two gravel paths in the course of wandering through a fine stretch of forest during which time your route gradually veers south, with tantalizing glimpses of a small lake in a forest clearing.

Where the trail crosses yet another gravel track, go left on it for more substantial views of the shoreline, attractively ringed as it is with lily pads. There is a small picnic area close by, providing a seat for resting while you contemplate Lost Lake, which you have just found.

On resuming, continue south on your path, then swing sharp right at the first T (unless you wish to find yourself in the municipal works yard). Stay with this path over two intersections on what has become a sawdust trail. Now the sports fields come into sight again, but your hike is not over yet; the climax is Mundy Lake itself.

To reach it, walk north again along the east side of the playing fields until you emerge at your objective's south end. A trail leads right round this oval body of water and it is worthwhile making the circumambulation for the varied views as well as for the sight of its flowers and plants: Labrador tea and tiger lilies in particular. Thereafter make your way back to your car having completed only one of the possible circuits in this attractive area, the colour codes to various trails providing you with the possibility of working out a circuit of your own on a subsequent visit.

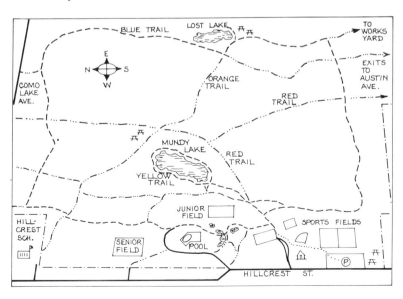

EAST OF VANCOUVER

52 JUG ISLAND BEACH

Round trip 5.2 km (3.2 mi)
Allow 2 hours
Old logging roads
Good all year

Now that the Greater Vancouver Regional District controls a fair amount of the peninsula extending north from Belcarra and separating Indian Arm from Bedwell Bay, you have the chance to walk to this most attractive beach at its north end, one from which you have striking views of the island-studded fiord with its mountain backdrop. The route itself, mostly old logging road, dating back in some instances to horse-powered operations, gives a few tantalizing glimpses of the coastline, but this is an all-or-nothing walk with the best saved for its destination.

For the beginning of the trail, turn left on Ioco Road from Highway 7A at the eastern end of Port Moody and follow it to Ioco School, where you turn right for Belcarra. At the next fork, stay left on Bedwell Bay Road, pass Sasamat Lake—another popular recreation area—and, just where the road turns left for Belcarra Park, park in Lot No. 2 on its north side. The route begins just to the right of a tall cedar on the left side of the parking area, and along it you work your way north, a little to the west of the ridge spine, taking care to stay on the travelled trail. After some thirty minutes, stay left, and almost immediately afterwards you come on a road running at right angles. Go left on this road (right is private property).

Some 300 m along it, fork right onto another old logging track. (The gravel road you were on provides access to more private homes.) On this route you climb steadily for a short distance, then the track levels off before the final descent to your beach. Try to reach it at low tide; by so doing you have more scope for exploring, perhaps clambering over seaweedy rocks to the little point at its north end for wider views towards the mountains, or, if you prefer the works of man, the sight of private boats that ply the waters of Indian Arm.

Return is normally by the same route. If, however, you do not object to walking on a road, you may turn right when you reach the gravel road then, just above the waterside houses, go left and follow the access road back along the coast.

View north up Indian Arm

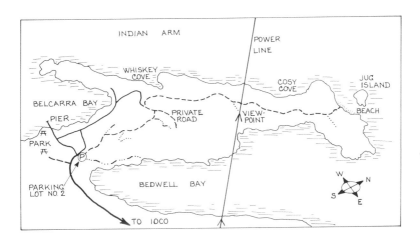

INDIAN ARM

POWER LINE

WHISKEY COVE

COSY COVE

JUG ISLAND

BELCARRA BAY

PRIVATE ROAD

VIEW POINT

BEACH

PIER

PARK

PARKING LOT NO. 2

BEDWELL BAY

W N S E

TO IOCO

119

North Beach, Mount Seymour (left) and Mount Elsay

EAST OF VANCOUVER

53 BUNTZEN LAKE

Round trip (longest circuit) 12 km
(7.5 mi)
Allow 5 hours
Service roads and trails
Good all year

Where do you have the choice of at least four delightful walks, ranging from a gentle stroll to a lung-opening circumambulation lasting several hours? The answer: Buntzen Lake, that attractive body of water, manmade though it is. Here, B.C. Hydro has done a superb job of creating recreational facilities: developed beach areas, launching sites for pleasure craft (no power boats), and trails for horse riders and hikers, the whole set in an impressive basin with tree-clad mountain slopes on either side.

To partake of what it has to offer, turn right at the Belcarra/Anmore fork beyond loco (see Walk 52), drive past the general store at Anmore, go right through the park gate (noting the hours of opening), and drive the unsur-faced road to the parking lot by South Beach. From here, to sample outings along the lake's east side, go right along the beach, cross a footbridge, and embark on an exceedingly fine forest trail that undulates gently as you proceed north.

The first possible destination if you feel lazy is a lakeside viewpoint that gives you a there-and-back outing of 2 km (1.2 mi), but if you are more ambitious, you may reach North Beach, approached by descending a flight of steps just after the intake tunnel that carries water from Coquitlam Lake on the other side of Eagle Ridge.

Here, at 4 km (2.5 mi) from your starting point, you may feel that honour is satisfied but if you do wish to complete the circuit follow the service road round the holding pond and past the great outlet pipe and dam, gradually bear left, then, near the road's low point go off left into the trees on a trail designated for both hikers and riders. This brings you to the west-side power line right-of-way, and along it you begin the return trip, with some interesting views of Swan Falls across the lake to raise the spirits. The trail remains more or less in the open at first, until about 15 minutes the horse route (Lakeview Trail) goes uphill to the right, while, as a hiker, you stay with the power pylons as they first descend into a hollow then climb up again over the next bluff. At this point, to avoid plunging down to lake level in some nasty bush around the shore of a bay, your trail goes sharp right into the forest just before pylon 15. Here, in the forest, the trail meanders along until eventually you reach a viewpoint over another small bay. Shortly thereafter you come to a fork and a choice between the "low road" that follows the shore through impressive forest and the "high road" that takes you up and over the next rise before bringing you back down to lake level where the two trails reunite just before you emerge beside a pumphouse.

Next you walk south on the service road, then cross a long wooden floating bridge spanning the lake's southern extension and the surrounding wetlands to the final lap through an attractive stretch of forest back to the south end of the parking area from which you set out.

A shorter walk on the lake's west side is, of course, possible as well by reversing the last part of the walk just described. Such an outing might take you out by the lakeside trail past the pumphouse, rising gently to the junction and returning over the top by going left at that point, this circuit giving you a walk of some 4 km (2.5 mi).

And the short outing at South Beach? For it, go left past the boat launching slip and head south to a knoll with a viewpoint along the whole length of the lake, once so appropriately called Lake Beautiful before it was renamed for a power company official.

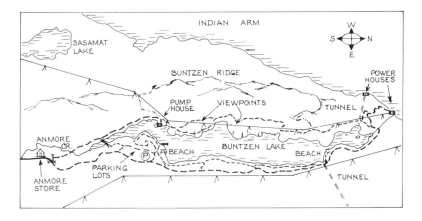

Woodpecker holes in cedar

EAST OF VANCOUVER

54 POCO TRAIL

Round trip (total circuit) 21.6 km
(13.5 mi)
Allow 6 hours
Dykes, trails, and sidewalks
Good all year

A few years ago, someone in Port Coquitlam conceived the bright idea of a circular walk round the municipality with transverse trails running east and west to link its two south-flowing rivers, the Pitt and the Coquitlam. Unfortunately, developments for both housing and commercial purposes have played havoc with the original design, especially over its southern half, so

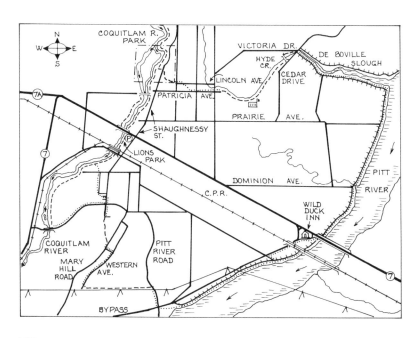

Pitt River marshlands

that, though the complete round is still possible, the sections that promise aesthetic satisfaction are those along the rivers, or, perhaps, the northern semicircle, especially if you can organize two cars, one at either end to save your having to retrace your steps.

If you do wish to make the complete round, a good start point is from Lions Park, situated a little south of Lougheed Highway on the east side of the Coquitlam River and reached off Shaughnessy Street just by a small shopping centre on its west side. From here, head south along the river dyke. Following this trail eventually brings you to Pitt River Road; however, since you would then have to walk back along this congested thoroughfare to its intersection with Shaughnessy, it may be best to bear left at the end of Wilson Street, cross a sports field, then travel south via Reeve Street and Saint George's to Central Park. Cross this recreation area and go left to reach Shaughnessy Street near the intersection where there is a traffic light.

Carry on south and, at road's end, pick up a trail that emerges on Mary Hill Road, make an uphill jog on Thea to Western Ave. and stay with this till you reach an east-west power line. Here you go left (east) over the height of land towards Pitt River. On the descent, because road and other developments have obliterated the original trail, turn right on Pitt River Road and follow it, crossing the new Mary Hill By-pass at the traffic lights to reach the riverbank. Now you turn northeast, negotiate the C.P. Railway, and just beyond the Wild Duck Inn, pass below the Highway 7 crossing of the Pitt River.

Continue north until you are forced westwards by De Boville Slough. From its head, work your way along Hyde Creek, first on its north side, later on its south bank. Next, travel along Patricia Avenue before cutting diagonally northwest to Lincoln. Another short jog north takes you again into woodland, but eventually you emerge on Shaughnessy once more. Cross this thoroughfare, enter the undeveloped municipal park beyond, and, having reached the Coquitlam River again, walk south along its bank to your starting point.

In preference to this marathon trail circuit (which is continually losing its signs to vandals), you may confine yourself to one or the other of the river walks, using Lions Park as the start of an outing along the Coquitlam River and the Wild Duck Inn for the Pitt River section.

To consider the former: Take the riverbank trail under the Lougheed Highway and continue north, a screen of trees on your right hiding the worst of the urban blight and allowing you to imagine the river as it must have been at one time. Next you pass a footbridge at the end of Patricia Avenue as you press on to where Poco Trail itself goes off right. The undeveloped municipal park beyond that turnoff has a number of unofficial trails; your rule, however, is to stay left, close to the stream. As you progress you may note that the waterway has some increasing claim to beauty, especially in periods of high water.

Eventually you find houses on your right, the privately developed Oxbow Estates whose own body of water justifies the title. A little beyond here, the route becomes bushy so, as there are now some pleasant spots beside the stream, you may make this your destination. Your view northwards is an interesting one of a U-shaped glaciated valley; to the east steep cutbanks bear mute testimony to the power of water.

Note that you may vary your return on this trip of 7.5 km (4.7 mi) by crossing the footbridge mentioned earlier to the river's west bank, following the dyke down that side and returning across the Lougheed Highway bridge to get back to your means of locomotion.

If you wish to travel north on the Pitt River section, turn south off Lougheed just west of the bridge and park close to the bank near the Wild Duck Inn. From here, all you need do is stay on the dyke top and enjoy the views of the polder lands to the east, set as these are against the summits of Golden Ears, stretching northwards to the great rampart, distant and majestic, of the aptly named Remote Peak.

Thus you continue to De Boville Slough, perhaps turning at its mouth for a total round trip distance of 7.2 km (4.5 mi), or walking to its head at Cedar Drive, so adding fully 3 km (nearly 2 mi) to the distance covered. You may note that from the intersection of Victoria Drive and Cedar, you have the possibility of yet another walk along the slough's north bank if you wish to explore farther up the Pitt River (see Walk 55).

All in all, despite a number of black spots, Poco Trail does give the possibility for some interesting outings if you are prepared to be selective.

Looking upstream on the Coquitlam River

Looking towards Minnekhada

EAST OF VANCOUVER

55 ADDINGTON MARSH

Round trip 7.6 km (4.7 mi)
Allow 3 hours
Dyke
Good all year

If plans by the Fish and Wildlife Branch of the Environment Ministry work out, this is a walk with a future, for officials hope, eventually, to install a trail system over much of the area; in fact, they are waiting only for it to be given official wildlife management status before proceeding. But it has a present also, for, even though it now ends part way along the southern boundary of the marsh, there is plenty to see and do as you stroll along quiet dykes, enjoying the Pitt Valley's rich variety of views.

From Lougheed Highway in Port Coquitlam, turn north off Coast Meridian Road for 2.4 km (1.5 mi) then go right on Apel Road. Where the road meets Victoria Drive, stay on the right fork and continue downhill to Cedar Drive, just where a dyked waterway—De Boville Slough—heads off east. Park by the gate on its north side (its south bank is a stretch of Poco Trail).

Noting that you may find cattle wandering along your route, you set off along the north bank of this waterway, its wide verges clad in coarse grass and contained by dykes set quite far back, the tops giving sustenance to numerous clusters of brambles, if you are looking for an autumn harvest. Nor are the dykes monotonously straight; instead they curve attractively, the artistic effect heightened by the still waters below the dyke on your left and the background of mountains.

Continuing down-channel, you pass a small marina on the slough's south side; your bank, however, is pleasantly unspoiled as you approach the main waterway of the Pitt River with its log booms and sandbanks, the latter even building up small islands here and there. By now you have turned northeast and have left most signs of human activity behind as you walk upstream; Sheridan Hill is across the river to your right front, a quarrying operation at its north end.

By now, waterfowl are plentiful. The great blue heron wings its leisurely way across the water, while on the dyke top and its sides the flicker dines off insects or darts for the trees at your approach. Thus you wander along, now looking across the water meadows to your left to the great swell of Burke Ridge, again enjoying the sight of the Golden Ears peaks rising behind the ridges of UBC Research Forest.

Finally comes the gate at the beginning of the marsh where there is a custodian's house and here for the time being your walk ends, a respectable outing but one that may be much richer in possibilities before long, especially during the spring and fall bird migrations.

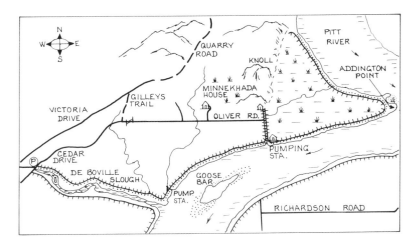

EAST OF VANCOUVER

56 MUNRO LAKE

Round trip 8 km (5 mi)
Allow 4 hours
High point 840 m (2750 ft)
Elevation gain 762.5 m (2500 ft)
Forest trail
July to October

The objective of this invigorating hike is an attractive little lake on a shoulder of Burke Mountain at a height of 840 m (2750 ft). It is invigorating because the trail, ascending quite steeply, makes few concessions to human frailty, so it is not for those who are in less than fair shape. On the other hand, the walk provides a good test of fitness as well as inspiring views across Pitt River lowlands to Golden Ears with Mount Baker and the Fraser Delta in sight for the return journey.

Driving east on the Lougheed Highway through Port Coquitlam, cross the Coquitlam River and continue to Coast Meridian Road. Turn sharp left here and travel north for 2.4 km (1.5 mi) to Apel Road. Go right at this junction then take the left branch of Victoria Drive just at the top of a hill and follow it in a northeasterly direction as it changes its name to Quarry Road and loses its blacktop surface, becoming somewhat pot-holey thereafter. On your way along this stretch, notice a rarity on the left of the road: a drystone wall of a type common in Scotland but not often seen in British Columbia. After nearly 7.2 km (4.5 mi) from the turn off Coast Meridian Road comes the parking place, a wide stretch on the left of the road where an old logging track comes downhill to join it.

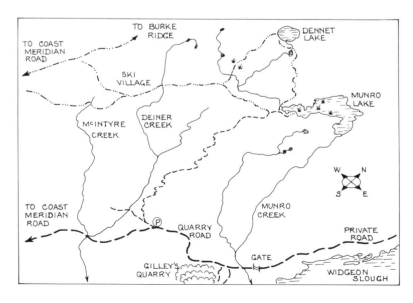

Munro Lake before draining

Follow this old road for about five minutes, then go right on the narrow footpath that rises steadily, a creek on its left. Now it is that conditioning begins to tell. The trail goes up quite steeply, heading mainly northwest with few alternations of gradient for something like 625 m (2000 ft). Part of the way leads through an old burned-over stretch, now in the process of being hidden by vigorous second growth, but there are still viewpoints, which give a valid excuse for resting while looking over Pitt River lowlands—a striking contrast to the alpine country round Golden Ears Mountain and Edge Peak.

Finally tree cover reasserts itself as you reach the shoulder of Burke Ridge and from now on the walk is virtually on the level; however, since nothing is perfect in this imperfect world, the trail is now muddy. A little south of the lake, another trail joins from the left, this one coming from Burke Mountain Village. Just at the south end of the lake, yet another trail goes off left, this one to Dennett Lake, higher and a good deal farther.

To find a place to rest, follow the path northwards along the lake's east bank to Munro Creek, the lake's outlet where you will find the remains of a small dam. Drinking water may be available here providing earlier arrivals have not messed up the area. Remember: Garbage breeds garbage; practise control. Lowering of the lake level has reduced the opportunity for fishing; be content, therefore, to contemplate the peaceful scene and enjoy the silence.

For the return trip, follow the same route, being careful to take the left fork where the Burke Mountain Trail, marked with aluminum circles, goes straight on towards the southwest, while your path is the one to Quarry Road. Now there is no strain; the difficulty is in restraint, so stop occasionally to feast the eyes on the great expanse of country that stretches south across the Fraser away to the border; Mount Baker stands as sentinel on the American side, its snow-clad slopes contrasting with the lush green of the lowland valleys.

Heading northwest towards Golden Ears

FRASER VALLEY NORTH

57 LOWER PITT RIVER

Round trip (up to) 16 km (10 mi)
Allow 4.5 hours
River dykes
Good all year

This is one of those delightful outings that may be tailored to suit almost any taste, from a 16-km (10-mi) out-and-back march for the tigers to a gentle stroll lasting less than an hour for lesser mortals; its highlight: the confluence of the Pitt River with the lordly Fraser. A bonus on the return north is the succession of eye-filling mountain vistas, from Seymour in the northwest to the mighty Golden Ears peaks that dominate the northern skyline.

For the longest walk, go left on Dewdney Trunk Road a short distance east of the Lougheed Highway's crossing of Pitt River. Follow Dewdney for almost 2 km (1.2 mi) then go left on Reichenbach Road, which brings you back towards the river and one possible starting point just before the end of blacktop where a gate on your left gives access to the dyke. You may, however, continue a little farther north to the marina by the mouth of the

Alouette River before you start your trek southwards. As you progress, you have the joy of bird-watching, from red-winged blackbirds to Canada geese, with herons added for good measure.

Soon you find yourself facing the Lougheed Highway but rather than scuttling across it, taking your life in your hands (or rather your feet), turn sharp right along the edge of the embankment to walk underneath the bridges, coming on another parking area between them. (This one is reached from the highway by turning back sharp right just at the east end of the crossing and, of course, from it you may walk either north or south according to inclination.) Continuing, however, you next must negotiate the C.P. Railway crossing, then, by a pumping station, comes another access point from Kennedy Road.

On this next stretch, views of the river are intermittent, a band of fine trees blocking uninterrupted views; however, you may enjoy the Dutch-like flat land to the left until you reach the meeting of the waters, a delightful spot for picnicking or just viewing the busy river scene, the distant Port Mann Bridge providing an interesting backdrop, while opposite are the trees and houses of Mary Hill. Even so, you may continue upstream on the Fraser itself, passing the end of Ford Road, another entry point, as you make for Pitt Meadows Airport. Just before this, however, your trip terminates at a cedar products mill, the ominous warning on its gate announcing that it is patrolled by attack dogs.

The return journey features the alpine views mentioned earlier, particularly spectacular in spring when the sun lights up the snow, inviting you to "lift your eyes unto the hills."

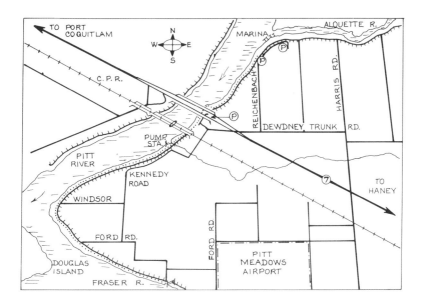

58 CHATHAM REACH

Round trip 12 km (7.5 mi)
Allow 3.5 hours
River dyke and taped route
Good all year

Pitt River with its succession of open dykes offers many fine outings, and this one must rank high on any aesthetic scale. Nor are you entirely confined to the riverbank; the north end of your walk has a nice little hill, attainable with a short scramble and giving some superb upriver views. You have a choice of distance as well: a short trip of 5.2 km (3.2 mi) and another one of practically double that length, the latter providing you with a stretch of the Alouette River for good measure.

For the shorter excursion, turn north off the Lougheed Highway on Dewdney Trunk Road a little east of the Pitt River Bridge. Go left at the T-junction with Harris Road and drive to the end of that thoroughfare at the river dyke, crossing the Alouette River en route. Once afoot, you turn right and head upstream, the views across to Addington Point and along Widgeon Creek opening out as you advance.

The longer walk involves your parking at the bridge over the Alouette, the best spot being on its south side. Your walk begins, therefore, with your crossing to the north bank, prior to setting off westwards downstream. As you proceed, you have hobby farms below you on your right, then, as you approach Pitt River, a variety of houseboats and small pleasure craft on the water to your left.

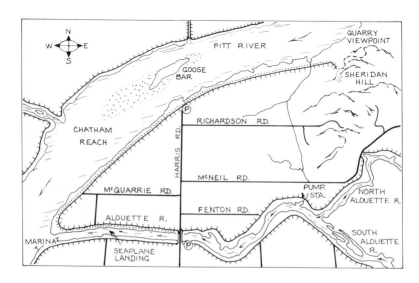

Peaceful scene on the Pitt River

Having arrived at the confluence of the tributary with the main stream, you begin your northward march along the Pitt, its shores dotted with log booms and its waters providing passage for tugs and small boats. After a walk of some thirty-five minutes, you pass the starting point of the shorter walk and acquire a feeling of smugness in the thought of the extra exercise you are getting. Proceeding, you turn a little east of north when the dyke begins to converge with Sheridan Hill, eventually coming to an end underneath its rock face.

From here, however, a taped trail heads off left, doubles back a little amid small timber, then gives you a short ascent to a viewpoint on the hill's west flank, one that commands a fine outlook to the north and west. The taped route itself goes on for another 800 m, taking you north to commanding views above a quarry, the loading dock of which was visible from the dyke.

Now the whole of the upper valley is spread out before you, from Burke Ridge and Widgeon Peak in the west to Pitt Lake lying due north, and to the east, the summit of Golden Ears towering majestically heavenward, fine at any time of the year but particularly striking when crowned with snow. One warning though: When the quarry is operating, there may be blasting; it is probably better, therefore, to save this trip for a weekend.

After such views as you have had, you may find the return a little anticlimactic once you have returned to the flat. Still, the countryside has a quiet pastoral beauty of its own, and urban blight seems far off as you retrace your steps to where you left your vehicle.

FRASER VALLEY NORTH

59 PITT POLDER DYKES

Round trip 12 km (7.5 mi)
Allow 4 hours
Dykes
Good much of the year (but remember the nesting season)

Choose a clear day for this walk to experience the full beauty of the majestic peaks enclosing the valley that houses Pitt Lake and the river draining from it. This is especially true in spring when the mountains are still snow-clad and when your way is sweetened by the scent of balm from the surrounding cottonwoods.

To reach the start of your outing, begin by going north on Dewdney Trunk Road and Harris as for the walk to Chatham Reach (see Walk 58). Fork right off Harris on McNeil, this road taking you east along the south end of Sheridan Hill. Thereafter you go left again on Rannie Road to reach your parking spot at the outlet from Pitt Lake, some 17.5 km (11 mi) from the main highway.

At the road's end with its locked gate, and opposite the public boat-launching ramp, a dyke—Pitt Polder's northern limit—runs along the south shore of the lake. Make your way along this, noting the occasional small craft in Grant Narrows, the shorebirds and waterfowl, and enjoying the mountain vistas.

At the east end, turn right on a dyke that runs south, then, after some twenty minutes, stay first right, then go left some ten minutes later where the treed right fork (very rough) goes back to the boat-launching ramp from which you started. Note, however, that the wildlife branch of the Ministry of

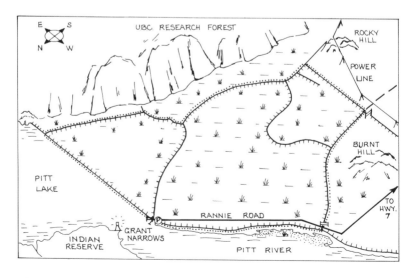

Grant Narrows

Environment has plans for upgrading this dyke, giving the possibility of a shorter circular outing. Continuing south, you pass a new dyke and arrive at a fork, with a drivable dyke top to the left. Stay left here, but some eight minutes later go right again, travelling for another fifteen minutes or so to a crossroads where dyke-top roads go off left to the south and straight ahead to the west.

Here turn right once more, working north and northwest. (Note: This area is off-limits during the sandhill crane nesting season from March to June.) Now you have fine views across the polder and into the valley of Widgeon Creek as you remain on this dyke till you return to the road you drove along en route to the lake outlet.

This you cross and follow a grassy track for a short distance to the dyke above the Pitt River, noting that this approach alone gives you access, a deep ditch blocking the way elsewhere. Now turn right to make your way back to the confluence of river and lake, continuing to enjoy the varied views as you proceed. Surely this area with its combined Dutch and alpine features must rank high on any list of Lower Mainland beauty spots.

Perhaps you may feel that the total round trip here described is a trifle lengthy. If so, you may easily accomplish the part of it that runs along the south end of the lake for a total walk of 5.6 km (3.5 mi) by retracing your steps instead of turning south.

Old donkey engine

FRASER VALLEY NORTH

60 UBC DEMONSTRATION FOREST

Round trip (blue trail) 7 km (4.5 mi)
Allow 2.5 hours
Trails and forest roads
Good much of the year

If you want a first-hand look at various aspects of forestry management, the installation near Haney administered by the Forestry Faculty of the University of British Columbia provides a perfect open-air classroom. For practical training, students come to the Research Forest of which this is part, but though its purpose is mainly academic, it does not neglect the general public, and even the casual visitor may find much to see and do, either alone or on a guided tour, or by participating in an open-house display of forestry expertise.

To reach the gate from the Lougheed Highway in Haney, turn north on 228th Street, go right on Dewdney Trunk Road for four blocks, then left on 232nd, following the Golden Ears Park signs for about 4 km (2.5 mi) until, a short distance beyond the bridge over the South Alouette River, you continue straight ahead as the park road goes right. Thereafter you have only a slight jog right onto Silver Valley Road before the forest car park. At the entrance are displays, a large map, and a list of rules: only hiking allowed, no dogs permitted (they worry the deer), and so on. From the office to the left of the gate, you may obtain maps and booklets on weekdays; on weekends during the summer you may also participate in a guided tour (phone 463-8148 or write R.R.2, Maple Ridge, B.C. V2X 7E7 for details).

To enjoy the forest's highlights on your own, you may follow one or other of the marked trails: red, yellow, and blue (with a short shelterbelt trail for seniors). The short red trail takes about an hour; yellow has the most detailed information, with an explanatory booklet available, and you will want some two hours to cover its 3.5 km (2.2 mi); blue is primarily a hiking trail, doubling the length of yellow and giving the greatest variety of scenery.

If your main interests are the forest and its management, you may follow the yellow trail; its twenty-one marked stops draw your attention to tree types, to tree breeding programs, and to the effects of forest pests. The final item, a refurbished donkey engine salvaged by students from its resting and rusting place by Pitt Lake, stands here in all the glory of a fresh coat of paint just as in its days of active service, which date back over sixty years to when its cheery whistle was first heard.

The blue trail branches left from the yellow and red shortly after crossing a forest road, thence it continues in fine open forest, makes its first crossing of Spring Creek, and breaks into the open before dropping briefly to Road G for its initial crossing of Blaney Creek, a little below a fish hatchery. Now you follow the creek upstream on its west bank, swing over to its east side and rise to cross another forest road, then start to turn eastwards above a cleared area where you enjoy a wide outlook to west and south. Next you pass a deer lookout on your right, cross yet another road, and finally link up with the yellow trail, going right at the junction to complete your circuit on the combined route.

A green trail, 2.4 km (1.5 mi) in length, has been created recently to allow exploration of the southeastern corner of the forest on both sides of the North Alouette River, the crossing of which was made possible by the construction of the Mills Bridge by the 1983 graduating class. For more information about the trail, enquire at the office or consult the map at the gate.

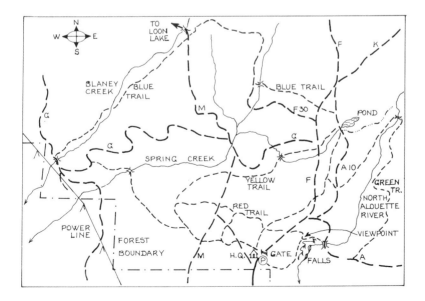

Devil's club in fruit

61 MIKE LAKE CIRCUIT

Round trip 5.6 km (3.5 mi)
Allow 2 hours
High point 460 m (1400 ft)
Elevation gain 180 m (600 ft)
Dirt road and park trail
Good March to November

If you have been sated with mountain and lake views, you may find this forest walk a restful change, for even if it does begin and end by Mike Lake, that is an unobtrusive body of water, itself dominated by tall trees. An advantage for the antisocial is that this section of Golden Ears Provincial Park is relatively unfrequented; only a few picnickers and canoeists, or hikers and climbers heading for Alouette Mountain or Blanshard Needle make use of the lakeside parking lot, though horseriders, too, may tie up at the hitching rack nearby.

To reach the start of this walk, drive into Golden Ears Park, following the signs north from Haney. From the park entrance, drive 4.5 km (2.8 mi) along the main access road, then turn off left at the park headquarters sign. Go left

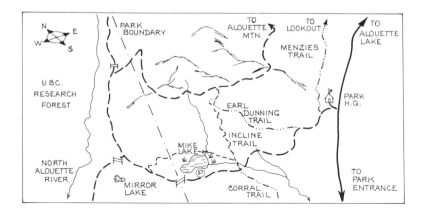

Mike Lake in winter

again after a few metres and travel on a dirt road for just over 1.6 km (1 mi) to the parking area by the lake, some 200 m beyond the point where Incline Trail goes off right. Just west of the car park a locked gate bars the road to vehicles, thereby ensuring peace for your walk along it.

Almost immediately, you lose the lake and are into trees, good-sized conifers for the most part, belonging to the UBC Research Forest, in which you are now walking. Continue westwards, staying right where another road comes uphill to join yours after some fifteen minutes, a process you repeat at the next fork where there is a locked gate to your left. As you walk this stretch, you become aware of the insistent sound of water far below you on your left—the North Alouette River.

Finally your route turns sharp right at a point where you see Mount Blanshard towering above trees (your only mountain view). Now you are heading back east, rising a little as you go till you come to the park sign for Alouette Mountain and you recognize your return route, Incline Trail, dropping sharp right downhill.

On this stretch, you speedily lose the height that you gained so gently in the earlier part of your sylvan stroll. The only thing to watch for on the trail is its junction with Eric Dunning Trail coming up from the left; you may, in fact, have seen its lower end signposted as you drove in. When you near your destination, you come on an interesting instance of drowned forest on your right, perhaps the result of beaver activity, a colony of these industrious creatures being located by the lake, the outlet of which you cross en route to the road.

For a shorter outing, you may use a recently constructed trail to go round the lake itself. From the parking lot, walk back to Incline Trail, cross the creek, then go left at the first fork.

Crossing the bog

FRASER VALLEY NORTH

62 ALOUETTE NATURE LOOP

Round trip 6 km (3.7 mi)
Allow 2.5 hours
High point 245 m (800 ft)
Elevation gain 95 m (300 ft)
Park trails
Good March to November

What title do you give a walk that embraces sections of no fewer than five trails in Golden Ears Provincial Park: Spirea, Bog, Lookout, Menzies, and Loop? Our suggestion, as above, takes account of the fact that part of the route is on the lower slopes of Alouette Mountain, that it provides a circuit, and that much of it is a self-guiding nature trail, the placards increasing your knowledge of forest lore as you walk along. Add to those things, interesting stretches of marsh complete with sphagnum moss and skunk cabbage, a

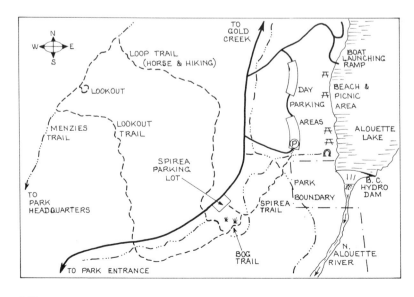

Sunday at the lake

fifty-year-old forest of hemlock that restored the tree cover after fire had devastated the valley, a lookout over Alouette Lake, and even a picnic table by its shore at the end of your outing, if you so desire.

For the beginning of this intriguing mixture, follow the signs for Golden Ears Park north from the east end of Haney, then continue 7.2 km (4.5 mi) beyond the park entrance to a right turn into a day-use area, noting as you pass, the Spirea Nature Trail parking lot about a kilometre before, a possible alternative starting point if you wish a shorter walk. In the day-use lot, park as closely as possible to the south end at which you enter; your trail is on the opposite side of the access road and it first takes you through nice open forest, rising a little in the process.

After some twenty minutes, you come to a fork where the trail from the Spirea parking lot joins and now you are on Bog Trail where, on boardwalks, you cross what would otherwise be very muddy ground. Shortly thereafter, you begin to turn right, cross a horse trail then the main access road, and start rising on Lookout Trail, again in forest. This trail is joined by Menzies Trail coming up from your left and, soon after, a clearing to your right provides the view over the lake and towards Mount Crickmer that you enjoy from a seat on a nice little bluff.

Continuing, you seek out a bridle trail coming uphill from the right for your descent, bringing you back to the main road a short distance before the Spirea Trail parking lot. Cross the road and join the trail on the side you started from, and now you retrace your steps over the bog and back to your starting point, staying right at the Spirea Loop fork.

Back at your car, you can drop down to the beach picnic area to refresh yourself; you may find all its tables occupied, though, on a fine summer weekend, for it is a popular area with the Greater Vancouver residents.

Alouette Lake and Mount Crickmer

FRASER VALLEY NORTH

63 VIKING CREEK LOOKOUT

Round trip 5 km (3.2 mi)
Allow 2 hours
High point 375 m (1200 ft)
Elevation gain 225 m (720 ft)
Park trail
Good March to November

This energetic outing provides a nice late-afternoon appetite rouser if you are camping in Golden Ears Park; it is also, however, suitable for the day visitor eager for some exercise, and it provides fine views over Alouette Lake and up the valley of Gold Creek, as well as more distant vistas to the south and west.

Having followed the park signs from Haney, drive from the entrance along the main access road for 11.6 km (7.2 mi) and, staying left at the campground fork, go left again for the West Canyon parking area. From here, you proceed north for about ten minutes on West Canyon Trail, the climbers' route to Golden Ears Mountain, until, after crossing a creek, you come on a marker pointing uphill to the left. This is your footpath. Though you rise steadily, the trail is suitable for warm weather walking, lying as it does in the shade of tall trees. The grade, too, is easy as the track swings from one side to the other, the creek you crossed being its southern boundary.

As you climb, you begin to get glimpses of the lake through the trees, but only after you have climbed to 330 m (1000 ft) do you have your first uninterrupted view. Here, just after the track has swung away from a large rock, a small level stretch, wired for protection, gives you a chance to draw breath while looking east and north.

Proceeding upwards, you next cross the creek that you saw earlier. By now the steepness of the slope above and the steep rock walls make it a perfect sun-trap, another pleasant stopping point for a short rest. Thereafter, the route first rises then levels off on a kind of bench among trees so that it is well back from the steep edge with its drop-off.

Finally, you reach the viewpoint, a clearing on a small rounded rock from which the southern half of the lake is laid out in front of you as far as the dam that controls its outflow to the South Alouette River, allowing diversion of its waters via a tunnel to Stave Lake and its hydro power stations. Away to the southwest, faint in the distance, are the outlines of the San Juan Islands of Puget Sound; across the lake is the logged-off ridge—best viewed when its raw nakedness is hidden under snow—that culminates in Mount Crickmer.

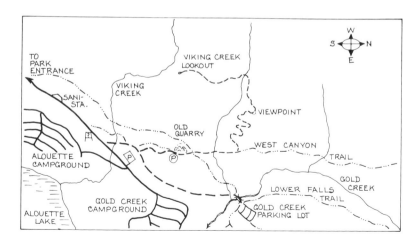

FRASER VALLEY NORTH

64 GOLD CREEK

Round trip to upper falls 7.2 km (4.5 mi)
Allow 2.5 hours
High point 250 m (800 ft)
Elevation gain 95 m (300 ft)
Park trail
Good April to October

Removal by the park authorities of the popular Burma Bridge means that this walk, for the time being at least, can be along only one side of the creek, and that being so, the Falls Trail on the east side is the more attractive. For the start of this outing, you first make for the entrance to Golden Ears Park from Haney, then, from the gate, drive just over 13 km (8.1 mi) on the main park access road, staying left at the campground fork and right at the West Canyon turnoff, and continuing on the gravel road across Gold Creek to parking on its north side.

From the west side of the parking area, follow the marked Lower Falls Trail. Your route, pleasantly timbered, runs parallel to the creek, giving you tantalizing glimpses of it through the trees. Eventually you do come close to it at a small beach where the flow is peaceful and the limpid stream a temptation for a dip on a hot day.

Again you lose sight of the creek as you proceed, but gradually you become aware that the sound of water has changed to a strong rushing. And here you are at the spray enshrouded and powerful lower falls. Your view westwards is awe-inspiring too, for you are looking directly at the great cirque formed by the mountain wall between Blanshard Needle and Edge Mountain, with Evans Peak standing, a lonely sentinel, to the south. Your round trip to here is 5.4 km (3 mi), and two hours is a liberal estimate of the time required.

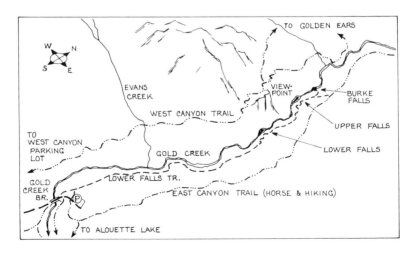

Burke Falls

To go farther, follow the track upstream for another 400 m to the even more spectacular upper falls where, safe behind a rail, you look straight down into the boiling waters in the canyon below a vertical drop, over which the creek hurls itself headlong.

This may well be your turning point; it is possible, however, to go farther on a rough trail to yet another cascade, Burke Falls, a destination that involves a short detour to the left off the trail, which itself continues and links up with the East Canyon horse trail, a one-time logging road. This, though a possible return route, cannot compare in interest with the track you used on your outward journey.

FRASER VALLEY NORTH

65 DAVIS LAKE

Round trip 4.8 km (3 mi)
Allow 2 hours
Trail and logging road
Good much of the year

Though this attractive body of water is listed as a provincial park, its surroundings remain virtually undeveloped, reached only by a road that is gravel for its last few kilometres and is used by logging trucks. Those of you who drive the 17.2 km (10.7 mi) along Sylvester Road from Lougheed Highway are, however, well rewarded for your trouble. Not only is there the lake; you also have MacDonald Falls to visit, where the waters of Murdo Creek tumble into a deep plunge pool, then continue to the valley floor in a series of rapids.

Coming east from Mission City, you drive 6.6 km (4.1 mi) beyond the traffic light at the junction of Highway 11 with Highway 7. Just before a small country grocery, your branch of Sylvester Road turns off sharply left, heading north a little to the east of Hatzic Lake, on the level at first but later hugging the side of the valley past farms and private homes. On your travels you pass Allan Lake—the name of which some enterprising developer is attempting to change to Alpen—and a short time later blacktop ends and you go forward on gravel.

About 14.5 km (9 mi) along you cross Cascade Creek, a pretty little Forest Service picnic site on its north bank being a possible stopping place for you on your return journey, especially if you wish to explore Cascade Creek Falls (see "Additional Walks"). After the creek your road starts to rise, hills close in on either side, and finally, after crossing Murdo Creek, there is a small parking area on the left from which a trail descends quite steeply past

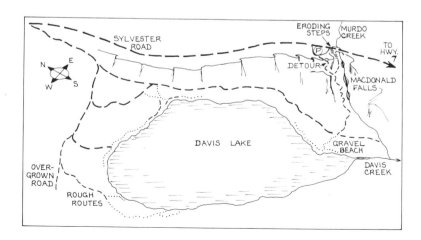

MacDonald Falls

the falls—spectacular in late spring. Then 90 m (300 ft) below your starting point you find yourself by the gravel shores of the lake's south end. Note, though, that the trail may have been washed out here and there, requiring care, especially on the descent.

You may, if you wish, walk the old logging road to the lake's north end; stay left at the intersection there and continue to a viewpoint looking south. You may also, should you desire to, return by the logging road's right fork, then go back uphill on Sylvester Road itself. This alternative may be dusty and busy with traffic, however, and it will probably be better to retrace your steps and face the steep ascent. One last point: If you drive to the end of the public road, you may walk to a viewpoint overlooking Salsbury Lake on logging roads; this round trip of 11 km (6.9 mi) is, however, rather dusty and hot in summer.

Highland cattle

FRASER VALLEY NORTH

66 HATZIC DYKE

Round trip 12 km (7.5 mi)
Allow 3.5 hours
Dyke and river trail
Good all year

One of the most attractive dyke walks along the Fraser River lies south of the Lougheed Highway between Nicomen Slough and Hatzic. Here farmland and the brown flood of the river supply the foreground and some of the finest of the mountain ranges around the valley provide romantic contrasts to the quiet pastoral scene.

Drive east on Highway 7 to Sylvester Road, 6.6 km (4.1 mi) beyond the light controlling traffic at the Mission City bridge. Turn right on Sylvester and cross the Canadian Pacific Railway tracks, then go left on McKamie Road, the first fork. Continue to the dyke and drive 2.6 km (1.6 mi) from the main highway to where a gate bars further vehicle traffic. Park here and continue west on foot using the narrow dirt road atop the dyke.

As you proceed, your route turns from southwest to northwest, giving plenty of variety. Particularly enjoyable are views towards Golden Ears and Mount Robie Reid, especially in spring sunshine. Nor is the dyke totally isolated; two roads intersect it, one after about thirty minutes, the second some twenty minutes later. Finally your further progress is barred by the outlet of Hatzic Lake and it is time to retrace your steps. Actually, though, you may vary your return somewhat by dropping from the dyke top to the riverbank, which you can follow until you come to a fence.

On your return trip you have a nice variety of views, too. Across the river are the treed slopes of Sumas Mountain, and away to the east are the majestic peaks of the Cheam Range: Cheam itself, Lady Peak, Baby Munday—some infant that —and Welch. These mountains look particularly good in spring with the winter snow gleaming on them; added attractions are the willows coming into leaf and the fragrance of cottonwood. The river, too, is at its highest then.

A last thought, as you enjoy this walk or wait for a C.P.R. freight train to drag its interminable length past the crossing at the highway, is the implication of this defence line against the potential power of the river. This power showed itself in 1948 and may do so again if given appropriate conditions.

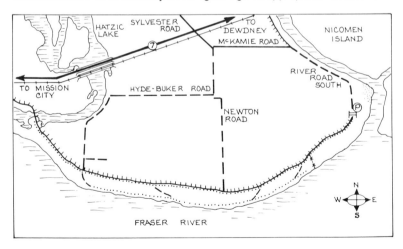

149

En route to Hemlock Valley

FRASER VALLEY NORTH

67 HEMLOCK VALLEY

Round trip (to ridge) 4.8 km (3 mi)
Allow 2 hours
High point 1400 m (4600 ft)
Elevation gain 400 m (1300 ft)
Service roads and trails
Best June to October

Though associated in the public mind mainly with winter activities, Hemlock Valley also offers a variety of interesting walks for the summer visitor, with choice of the valley bottom or an ascent to the western ridge as two alternatives, the latter providing a series of superb views.

The valley itself is reached by turning north off Highway 7 at the Sasquatch Hotel in Harrison Mills and driving 7.8 km (about 5 mi) before going left on the Hemlock Valley approach road after crossing the Chehalis River where there is a salmon hatchery and picnic site. The road, despite its warnings, has a nice grade and good surface for its 12.8 km (8 mi), rising in a series of bends that present interesting views over Weaver Lake before entering the downhill ski area development in the upper valley.

From the day lodge parking area at the road end, make for the green (Sasquatch) chairlift and use the service road and the grassy slope on its right to gain height. Because it is a little steep, the slope gives an opportunity for you to enjoy the developing vista as you stop for breath. If you think the view from the valley is good, you will be entranced by the one from the ridge, from which you look across to the Cheam peaks, Slesse, Tomyhoi, and Mount Baker. The views to the north and west are equally striking, from Harrison Lake round to Mount Robie Reid with the Chehalis Valley below you.

Nor are you confined to the top by the chairlift. You may walk northeast on a rudimentary trail for quite some distance, while another shorter ridge to the west is also attractive. It is possible, as well, that the Hemlock owners will put in a trail south to link up with the top of the red (Skyline) chair, so making a circular walk possible.

The little tributary basin to the south of the ski village also has possibilities, and a walking trail into it has been proposed, the approach being via Laurel and Larkspur off Hemlock Valley Road to the left as you go up-valley. It may, however, be a good idea to ask at the day lodge for particulars, since construction is still going on and plans are subject to change.

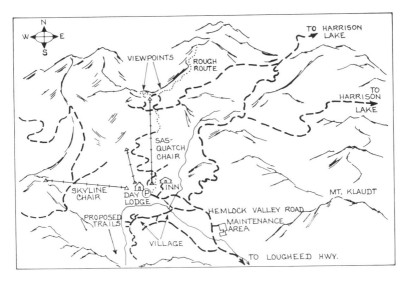

FRASER VALLEY NORTH

68 HARRISON LOOKOUT

Round trip 4.8 km (3 mi)
Allow 3 hours
High point 720 m (2300 ft)
Elevation gain 320 m (1025 ft)
Logging road and trail
Best June to October

This is a fine outing for you if you are holidaying in the Weaver Creek recreation area, though you may easily embark on the gravel road that runs along the west side of Harrison Lake and climb to the site of the one-time Forest Service lookout on a day trip from as far away as Vancouver. Certainly the breathtaking views over the lake make it well worthwhile.

As you do for Hemlock Valley, turn off Highway 7 at Harrison Mills; this time, however, you stay right where the ski area road branches off. Now you are on gravel and you recall the notice "USE AT YOUR OWN RISK" as you pass the Weaver Creek spawning channels, which are wild with piscine activity in the October of every fourth year when the sockeye return to spawn and die. A little beyond here are the turnoffs to forest campgrounds at Weaver Lake and Francis Lake, and now you have Harrison Lake itself spread out below you as you follow your roller-coaster road past Cartmell Creek, followed by Coral Falls. Next comes the sign for Wood Lake Campsite and almost 4 km (2.5 mi) beyond, you drop into a deep gully to cross Hale Creek; the sign left to Sunrise Lake is about 1.6 km (1 mi) farther on.

Your road, to the right, is some 300 m farther and you may either park by it or, if you wish, drive in a little way, after a total distance of 37.6 km (23.5 mi) from Highway 7. Once on foot, you cross a small stream, then at a fork in a recently logged area stay left on an old road—a little overgrown—and

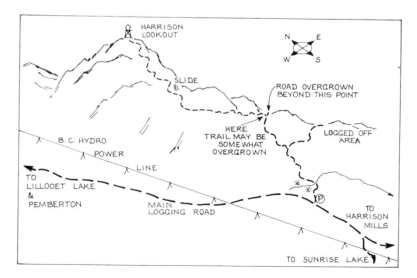

Harrison Lookout

start ascending to the east. The road finally becomes completely overgrown at its high point, where a steep, taped foot trail goes off left. As you climb, you catch occasional glimpses of the lake, then you breast the final rise and there is the lookout with its panoramic views.

Harrison Lake, 625 m (2000 ft) below you, is here split by Long Island, complete with its own smaller lakes. To the east are the ridges culminating in The Old Settler, while south are the majestic peaks of the Cheam Range, with Mount Baker beyond and to the right. Westwards, you have another group of snow-clad summits, and north, beyond the lake, are more towering giants lying east of Lillooet Lake.

Your return walk and the drive southwards along the lake have their own points of interest; note, however, that logging may be going on so save this outing for a weekend, or, if that is not possible, remember that logging trucks have right-of-way, as if their sheer size did not ensure that.

FRASER VALLEY NORTH

69 AGASSIZ LOOKOUT

Round trip (from corner)
3.2 km (2 mi)
Allow 1.5 hours
High point 665 m (2100 ft)
Elevation gain 62.5 m (200 ft)
Gravel road and trail
Good June to October

Mount Woodside and Mount Agassiz are two summits on a long ridge that lies between the Harrison River and Highway 9 running north from Agassiz to Harrison Hot Springs, with Highway 7 along its south end. The ridge also has an approach road that allows you to give your vehicle an amount of exercise inversely proportional to the amount you get yourself. How far up this road you drive depends on your attitude towards your car's well-being, and of course the power of its motor. You will want to drive some way, however, if only to avoid the need for slogging along a logging road on a warm summer day.

Travelling east on Highway 7 some 4.9 km (3 mi) beyond Harrison River Bridge, and just before Mount Woodside Cafe near the top of a long hill, you go left on a gravel road. This route rises in a series of S bends and its steepness requires a little care, especially as you may meet members of the hang-gliding fraternity who use it as an approach to a jump-off point from the sixth bend, a possible parking spot for you, too.

Here, just over 3 km (1.9 mi) from the start of your road, you have a fine view over the Harrison River and west along the Fraser itself. From this point proceed nearly 1 km (0.5 mi) along the straight stretch until you come on a slightly overgrown old road forking right. Follow this till it peters out a short distance before the foot of an old fall of rocks, from which point a faint trail takes you across the talus and upwards, gradually circling back to the west.

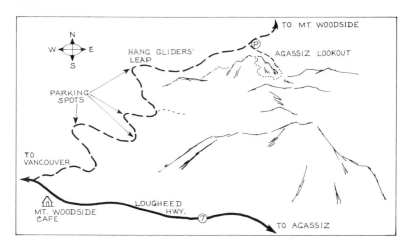

Across the Fraser to Mount Cheam

Once you are round on the south side of the knoll, your route rises straight up to the summit above, the destination of your outing. From this minor peak you have a striking view of Mount Agassiz as you look north along the ridge; even more striking, however, is the view across the Upper Fraser Valley from the highway crossing on the Rosedale-Agassiz bridge to the great peaks of the Cascade Mountains beyond.

Though short, this outing is for experienced hikers because of the roughness of the trail. The rewards, the aforementioned views, however, make it worthwhile if you do embark on it. Note also that with a suitable vehicle you can now drive all the way to the Mount Woodside repeater station, from which a short scramble brings you to an eminence overlooking the Harrison River to the west, and gives an unexpected view northwards to the lake.

Looking towards the Harrison Hot Springs Hotel

FRASER VALLEY NORTH

70 WHIPPOORWILL POINT

Round trip 5 km (3 mi)
Allow 2 hours
Trail
Good most of year

Next time you are at Harrison Hot Springs, take this short walk to put some space between the crowds and yourself. You may even find a swim-suit useful, for the route features a secluded beach, Sandy Cove, accessible only from this trail or by boat.

As a beginning, walk westwards along the esplanade fronting the beach and past the hotel in the direction of the hot springs. Here, where the naturally hot water (83° C), smelling strongly of sulphur, is collected in a great steaming tank to be piped to the village, the trail—somewhat rough at its beginning because of a small washout—starts rising uphill. Do not descend to the track on the beach; it goes only as far as the village pollution control centre and in any case, it may be partly submerged in periods of high water.

As you climb, you have quite a steep drop-off on your right; the trail, however, is perfectly safe if you take a little care. Next you have to double back to detour above a bluff where the original route used wooden stagings, now collapsed, and finally your route levels off some 30 m (100 ft) above the surface of the lake, but soon you find yourself walking into a valley apparently away from the water as you start descending.

Next comes the parting of the ways. If you go straight forward on the left-hand trail, you find yourself in a short time beside the Harrison River at an interesting spot but one that is a little short on space. The main route goes right, gently into the valley, and finally emerges on a beautiful little beach, the Sandy Cove already mentioned. Here you may relax at leisure if you wish or proceed the further short distance to the point. To do so, walk along the beach to its northwestern end and pick up the continuation of the trail as it runs into the trees, rising a little as it goes.

From the beach to the river outlet is only a few hundred metres, so you soon emerge from trees onto the picturesque rock point, adorned with a beacon and triangular navigation markers, which provides you with striking lake and mountain views as you look northwards. Above Harrison Lake's eastern shoreline is The Old Settler, a mountain more interestingly named than many others. Farther north is Mount Breakenridge with its surrounding glaciers, and away in the extreme distance is Cairn Needle, pointing skywards. Thus spiritually refreshed, you return to the world of men, the walk probably having done you at least as much good as the spa's mineral waters.

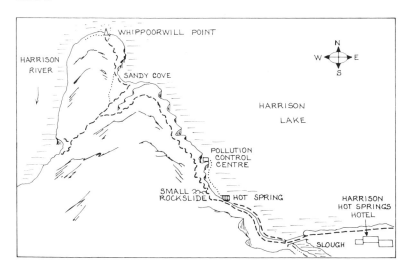

Fraser River view, Mount Seymour in distance

FRASER VALLEY SOUTH

71 BARNSTON ISLAND

Island round trip 9.6 km (6 mi)
Allow 3.5 hours
Road and riverbank
Good all year

One of Shakespeare's characters boasted that he could "call spirits from the vasty deep"; well, so can the would-be visitor to this island, for you may summon a ferry merely by sounding a car horn—the modern equivalent of a magic charm, though not so euphonious. In any event, this is how you reach the island, set in the Fraser River northwest of Langley.

To reach the sounding-off point from Highway 1, turn off on 176th Street North at the Clover Valley Interchange located about 7.2 km (4.5 mi) east of the Port Mann Bridge. After 1.6 km (1 mi) turn east on 104th Avenue (Hjorth Road), cross the C.N. Railway, and drive to the ferry stage. Actually you will not need your car on your island walk; you may, therefore, travel across on the free ferry as a foot passenger.

On disembarking, turn right and follow the road past some nondescript farm buildings where river access is barred by "No Trespassing" signs. Passing these you proceed for some thirty minutes to reach a swampy area in its wild state, an indication of what much of the island must have been like before dyking and draining. This swamp, in turn, gives way to a neater stretch of farmland, and another twenty minutes or so of walking brings you to a beach at the island's eastern extremity.

Here is a good spot for rest and refreshment before resuming your circumambulation, now on the riverbank itself. You may remain on the bank as you walk along the island's north side, the waters of the Fraser sliding silently by in almost sinister fashion on your right. Only once must you briefly break this pattern, ascending to the road to avoid a small farm. Otherwise you remain by the river, enjoying the airy perfume of the cottonwoods if you undertake this outing in spring.

From the island's northwest corner at Robert Point, you are back on the road, since this section is settled right to the water's edge. Perhaps, though, it is just as well that you do not have to watch your footing, for you are now looking directly at Mount Baker, with Twin Sisters on its right and the great peaks of the Cascades to the left, culminating in the Lucky Four and the Cheam Range.

As a contrast to the neat farmlands on the island across the water, you may enjoy a walk in the Surrey Bend area by going north from the mainland ferry dock along the shoreline on a trail (wet at times) that gives you a chance to experience undyked flood plain with its bog ecology, this stretch of riverfront being totally undeveloped except for drainage ditches designed to ease the threat of flooding. The route you are on gets you to a point just opposite the northwest tip of Barnston Island where a ditch blocks further progress. You may, however, return by another route alongside a canal that cuts directly south through the bog, coming out on 104th Avenue some 600 m inland, the total distance being about 5.5 km (3.5 mi).

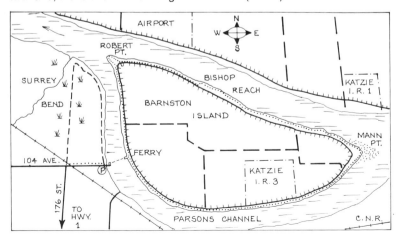

FRASER VALLEY SOUTH

72 FORT LANGLEY

Round trip 4 km (2.5 mi)
Allow at least 2 hours
Roads and footpaths
Good all year

Those who leave their cars, enter the fort, visit its buildings, then depart are missing a number of interesting features that this national historic park has to offer. To get the full sense of what living in such a situation was like, you should look at the surroundings as well, since these, down to the river frontage, put the fort in its context: a once-important Hudson's Bay trading post, established in 1839 on a high bank above the Fraser River.

The approach from Highway 1 is simple, with direction signs pointing the shortest route from the 200th Street Interchange, located 12 km (7.5 mi) east of the Port Mann Bridge. If you wish to get into the spirit of historical research, however, go left on 208th Street from 88th Avenue instead of continuing straight on. By so doing, you come to Allard Crescent, a road that follows the bend of the Fraser. Go right on this road and 4.3 km (2.7 mi) along it you find on the riverbank an unobtrusive cairn marking the site of the original fort, dating from 1827, nearly 5 km (3 mi) downstream from the present settlement.

From here, continue south and east, with a right turn followed by a left onto 96th Avenue (Wilson Crescent). By so doing, you come to Glover Road in the village proper, and from here a short left followed by a right on Mavis Avenue takes you to the parking lot by the park's administration building and ticket office.

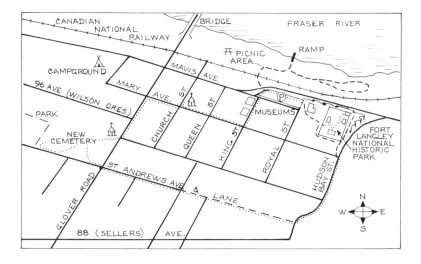

Old Fort Langley store

Inside the stockade on your right as you enter is the Big House, once the officers' quarters, now a museum; and don't miss the Southdown sheep in their pen behind. To your left as you emerge is the refurbished workshop and diagonally across the grounds is the store, the one original structure left standing. Enter it to marvel at the great selection of nineteenth-century trade goods it carried. Last of all, you come to the little bastion, with its nine-pound cannon guarding the river approach. These features are all described in the excellent booklet issued by Parks Canada and available at the Big House.

When you leave the fort, turn left and follow its stockade south then east till you stand on the high bank looking upriver above the flat farmland below you. Next, continue south on Hudson's Bay Street, passing the end of Francis Avenue then heading west along a lane that becomes Saint Andrew's Avenue as it approaches Glover Road. On the west side of this avenue is a graveyard, its older headstones proclaiming a variety of birthplaces for those who sleep peacefully below them.

Go north on Glover once more, this time turning east (right) on Mary Avenue for sight of the tiny Anglican church (Saint George's) beside which the small Pioneer Cemetery is marked by a monument. Two blocks on, turn left on King Street for more history, social this time, for here are located the B.C. Museum of Agriculture and Fort Langley's own Centennial Museum, the latter just across the road from the parking area. Before you leave, however, continue across River Road, pick up the footpath that traverses the C.N. Railway, and you find yourself on the river. Looking downstream you see the bridge that carries the road to Albion Ferry; straight across, the little white church of the Indian reserve gleams in the sun. Now you may walk along the bank of what was once the harbour before the upper limit of navigation moved upstream in 1858, the year that, ironically, saw Fort Langley's brief moment of political glory, when the colony of British Columbia was proclaimed there.

As you retrace your steps to the present, you may feel that you have travelled much farther than the distance covered, back to the mid-nineteenth century in fact, when life was stern and simple and the outside world far away.

Boardwalk between upturned roots

FRASER VALLEY SOUTH

73 ALDERGROVE LAKE PARK

Round trip 4 km (2.5 mi)
Allow 1.5 hours
Park trail
Good most of the year

Do not be misled by the word "lake" in the title. The body of water so designated is, in fact, a large outdoor swimming pool, created by damming a creek that runs in the pleasant pastoral valley along which this walk is located. You need not, therefore, go near the man-created recreation area unless you wish to; you may wander at leisure in surroundings that are natural except for the trail. Thanks to the activity of beavers, however, this path has had to be raised on a wooden walkway to allow for crossing a marsh.

As you travel east on Highway 1 beyond Langley, turn off right on Highway 13 and head south, going straight ahead at traffic lights where a left turn would take you into Aldergrove Village. Go left on 8th Avenue at the park directional sign, cross Jackman Road, and shortly after make a right turn into the park. On your way to the car park by the creek, note the information board on the right before you descend the hill; it helps mark your return route. Leave your car just across the creek; the trail is to the left of the bridge, heading east.

Once on foot, you proceed upstream in open forest, with varied wild flowers to test your powers of identification if you choose early summer for this outing. Gradually your route becomes boardwalk and along it you tramp, noting the interesting features of valley ecology. Finally you begin turning a little to the left, coming into the open for your crossing of the valley, here covered by quite a wide expanse of water, thanks to those natural engineers who were active long before B.C. Hydro started building dams.

On its north side, the valley is more open, and you enjoy views across it to the international boundary as you attain the level of the surrounding country-side. Now you are heading back west and, after crossing a stile, traversing another attractive stretch of forest. Next comes a fairly narrow ridge, after which you emerge on open meadow, the information board ahead of you. Before your descent, make a short detour left to a viewpoint atop a steep bank, then rejoin the trail into the valley, passing the group activity area as you approach the road again at the foot of the hill.

If you wish to see the lake, cross the road to make a short circular trip, out along the north side of the creek, over a bridge to its south side, going left at a T-junction and continuing round the lake on a nature trail before returning to your vehicle.

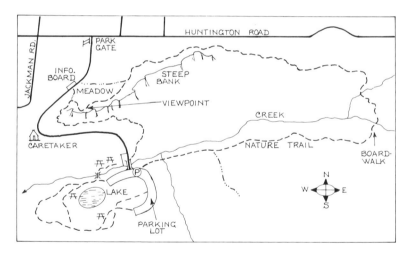

FRASER VALLEY SOUTH

74 MATSQUI DYKE

Round trip 19.3 km (12 mi)
Allow up to 6 hours
Dyke and roadway
Good all year

If you wish, you may stretch this into a there-and-back trip of some 19 km (12 mi); there are, however, a number of intermediate points at which you may turn around when you feel that you have had enough exercise along this section of the Centennial Trail in the Abbotsford area.

To reach the western end of this walk, leave Highway 1 at the Mount Lehman Road Interchange and drive north 4.8 km (3 mi) to Harris Road. Turn right, travel 3 km (2 mi) to Glenmore Road where you go left, and, after a few hundred metres, park at the end of the river dyke. As you look across the Fraser, you see Matsqui Island ahead of you, with Mission City on the opposite bank, the bell tower of its religious institution, Westminster Abbey, dominating the urban area.

Travel northeast at first along the dyke until after some fifteen minutes you arrive at the mouth of Matsqui Slough with its flood-control pumping station. From here you may use the road or the riverbank as you head towards the bridge connecting Abbotsford and Mission (Highway 11), which you reach after about an hour's walking. The bridge approach is, of course, just above you as you walk beneath the span, but just beyond, you come on the old highway, which used the C.P. rail bridge as a right-of-way.

If you continue beyond this point, your route may alternate between a track on the bank and the roadway behind as the curve of the river causes you to change direction from northeast to southeast, and brings Sumas Mountain directly into view. Finally, 9.6 km (6 mi) from your starting point,

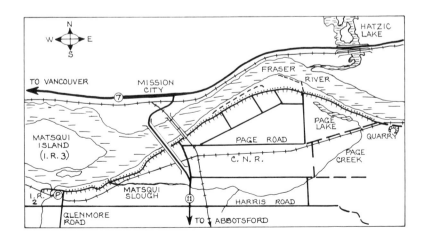

Mission road bridge

this dyke sections ends at its intersection with Page Road, shortly after passing a small lake on your right.

Thus your outward journey ends and unless you have been able to organize two cars, one at either end, you have the same distance to return. Incidentally, if this suggests a portage, it is entirely appropriate since *Matsqui* means "portage." The walking is not difficult, the dyke being virtually flat; it is nearly all in the open, however, and may be somewhat warm going on a summer's day.

FRASER VALLEY SOUTH

75 SUMAS MOUNTAIN PARK

Round trip 5 km (3.2 mi)
Allow 3 hours
High point 900 m (2950 ft)
Forest trail and dirt road
Good July to October

For an easy ascent with various bonuses, try this mountain set in the middle of the Fraser's lower valley and familiar to all who drive eastwards beyond Abbotsford along Highway 1. Not only do you start high, so reducing the amount of climbing you must do but you also go though beautiful forest—except for one litter-strewn picnic area—and past Chadsey Lake, itself embowered in trees. Then you have summit views over the flatlands with a mountain background that stretches from the Cheam summits to Mount Baker, dominant over the southern horizon.

From the provincial information centre 3 km (1.8 mi) east of Abbotsford, drive 2.6 km (1.6 mi) then turn left on Sumas Mountain Road, passing Kilgard with its brick and tile ovens and climbing fairly steadily for 8 km (5 mi), the road becoming gravel en route. At Batts Road, the sign for Sumas Mountain Park takes you off right, and on this road, rather rough at the time of printing, you switchback upwards for another 8 km (5 mi) until, at a hairpin bend, you come on a parking area to the left with a wooden sign indicating a trail for Chadsey Lake, though the road itself continues for another kilometre.

Since you are going to walk, not drive, to the peak, this is where you leave your vehicle. Do not be dismayed that the trail descends instead of climbing as you might expect; you will have time to regain lost height later, after your visit to the lake, reached by a walk through stately forest.

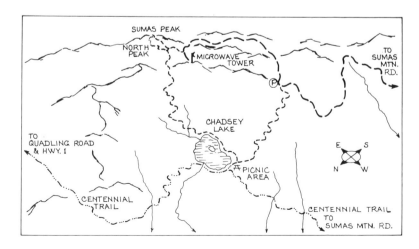

Southeast over the Fraser Valley

As you come down to this picturesque body of water, you see your route going along its shores to the right, on its south side to the southeastern corner, at which point you begin to climb in a series of wide S bends on a reasonably gentle gradient. You remain among trees and, as this is a north-facing slope, snow lingers into early summer so save this walk for late June or July. Finally, 245 m (800 ft) above the lake, the trees thin out, you arrive at a trail junction, and whether you go left to the north viewpoint or straight ahead to the main one is immaterial, as there are views from both that ought to satisfy the most critical, with mountain and valley laid out in front of you and antlike cars on the highway far below.

For your return, take the main trail back to the end of the road, which you walk back down as it goes first west, then north, to the parking place.

McNulty Falls

FRASER VALLEY SOUTH

76 McNULTY FALLS

Round trip 6.4 km (4 mi)
Allow 3.5 hours
High point 655 m (2100 ft)
Trail
Good June to October

Everyone who travels east along Highway 1 beyond Chilliwack must be familiar with Bridal Veil Falls at Popkum, graced as they are with provincial park status. Only 4.5 km (2.8 mi) farther east, however, the equally spectacular McNulty Falls are relatively unknown, not being visible from the road and lacking vehicle approach. A trail to them does exist, though, and some expenditure of energy also gives you a number of fine mountain and valley and lacking vehicle approach. A trail to them does exist, though, and some expenditure of energy also gives you a number of fine mountain and valley views as you zigzag your way up the spine of a ridge to the 655-m (2100-ft) level.

A little over 1 km (0.7 mi) beyond Julseth Road, a crossbar on the south side of the highway marks the trail beginning. At first it consists of a somewhat overgrown road but soon enters a clearing a little east of the creek. From here the marked route leads upwards through lusty thimbleberry bushes and soon comes to a power line right-of-way, also rather bushy; once back among trees, however, the undergrowth thins out as you continue your ascent, passing to the right of an old footbridge.

After about forty minutes of walking comes your first viewpoint up the main valley of the Fraser, and now you start rising more steeply until, some twenty minutes later, you have your first sight of the falls from a high commanding spur of rock. For more exercise and even more rewarding views, you may continue upwards, taking care at one point where a fallen tree (1982) has briefly obscured the route. Eventually, a good hour beyond the falls, you reach the main valley lookout, a few steps to the right of the trail.

From here you may enjoy views to the west and north, including the confluence of the Fraser and the Harrison. From here, too, you may look upwards to the steep bush-covered slopes, scarred here and there by winter avalanches or by the gullies of creeks tumbling from the snowfields of Mount Cheam.

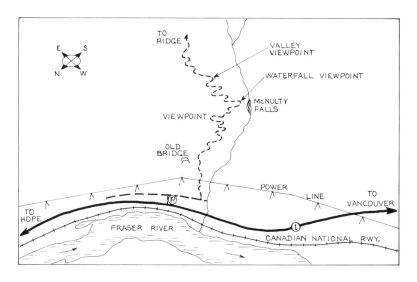

Pond near Vedder Mountain summit

CULTUS LAKE AREA

77 VEDDER MOUNTAIN

Round trip 11.1 km (7 mi)
Allow 4.5 hours
High point 940 m (3000 ft)
Elevation gain 312 m (1000 ft)
Old road and trail
Good May to October

Some people are content only with ascending every mountain from its base; if, however, you do not mind having your vehicle work for you, you may turn this into a civilized half-day ramble.

Your approach is via a dirt road from a right turn off the main highway to Cultus Lake just at the Ministry of Highways office, itself located 3.2 km (2 mi) south of the Chilliwack River bridge at Vedder Crossing. (The trail sign is high on a tree by the office entrance.) After about 800 m, take the right (uphill) fork; it is narrow, but quite passable for most cars on the 3.4-km (2.1-mi) stretch to where a rough jeep road forks right. From here you walk, following the right fork for less than fifteen minutes then going left for another ten before turning right once more on a footpath.

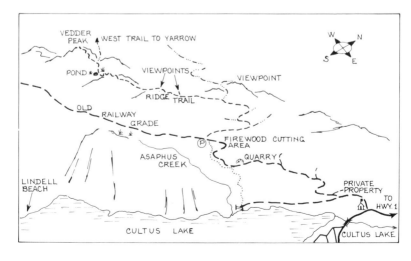

Across the ridge to the Cheam Range

For a time you are in pleasant open forest heading fairly gently uphill and turning gradually from north to west, ignoring a track to the right as the trail curves to run along the ridge, now garbed in thick second-growth forest. After about an hour's walking, you have a delightful viewpoint a few steps off to the right. From it you look across the Fraser Valley to the distant peaks to the north, particularly impressive when under snow. Next, after another 400 m comes a fine view to the east along the Chilliwack Valley with the Cheam peaks as a backdrop, while to the south a large glacier announces the west shoulder of Mount Baker.

As you proceed along Ridge Trail, you find yourself dropping suddenly to a little lake, well furnished with water lilies and surrounded by some marshy ground, before you start to regain height on your trek to the summit, meeting en route the West Trail, one that comes up from low on the Yarrow side, before the final climb with its bit of scrambling. The reward, uninterrupted views, makes everything worth the expenditure of energy, especially as you have at different times of the summer a variety of plants—violets and trilliums, pyrola, mosses, and mushrooms—to gladden the eye and enliven the way.

On the Seven Sisters trail

CULTUS LAKE AREA

78 SEVEN SISTERS TRAIL

Round trip 6 km (3.7 mi)
Allow 2 hours
Park trails
Good most of the year

Tired of water sports on Cultus Lake? Try this forest walk if you are staying in the provincial park or just visiting the area, having driven along the Columbia Valley Highway past the village of Cultus Lake to park at the south end of the Entrance Bay picnic ground.

From here, cross the little creek to the Jade Bay launch site, go left, cross the highway, and follow the campground road to just beyond campsite 7. Here, on your right, a flight of steps leads uphill to the trail to Clear Creek Campsite. Up you go till the route levels off in forest above the little valley that drains into Entrance Bay.

This is fairly old second-growth forest, certainly dating from the days when, after logging, tree cover was left to restore itself, resulting in a rather untidy mixture of trees, mainly deciduous, with conifers here and there. Through this area the trail wanders, rising and falling gently until, at the foot of more steps, you have a sign pointing uphill to a group of large Douglas-fir. These are the Seven Sisters, survivors of the original forest, somehow spared the fate of the rest of their family.

Having descended to the trail again after your inspection of these stately trees, you may feel that honour has been satisfied and that return is in order. If, however, you wish more exercise, continue southwards past another route coming downhill from the left and turn left only at the next junction, where the right fork goes into Clear Creek Campsite. Once again, now on one of the park's riding trails, you travel uphill to another T-junction, this one coming just before a creek. Here you go left once more, parallelling the creek for a short time then swinging away from it, still heading east.

Watch carefully on your left for a foot trail among some interesting moss-clad trees leading back to the intersection that you passed already. From here, you return by the original route, passing once more the grove of the Seven Sisters, then descending the steps to the campground.

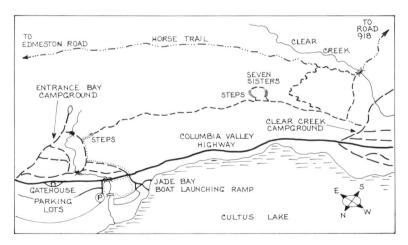

Crossing Watt Creek

CULTUS LAKE AREA

79 TEAPOT HILL

Round trip (route 1) 3.2 km (2 mi)
Allow 1 hour
High point 320 m (1000 ft)
Elevation gain 220 m (700 ft)

Round trip (route 2) 4.8 km (3 mi)
Allow 2 hours
High point 320 m (1000 ft)
Elevation gain 125 m (400 ft)
Trail
Good most of the year

When does one walk become two? Answer: When you can reach the same destination from entirely different starting points—either of which is a satisfactory outing on its own—though the two may be combined by adroit manipulation of transport. Such is the case with Teapot Hill, a 320-m (1000-ft) bump located just east of the southern end of Cultus Lake and situated in the provincial park of the same name some 11 km (7 mi) from Chilliwack.

The first approach, entirely within the park boundaries, goes off to the left some 2.6 km (1.6 mi) beyond Lakeside Lodge as you drive south along Columbia Valley Highway. Here, Road 918, a one-time logging track now gated to block vehicle access, leads uphill from a spot where there is parking space for several cars by the lake. The route rises steadily but on a fairly gentle grade, close to a creek at first but later in mixed forest, the trees dense here and there, the lush growth of fern and moss indicating a plentiful rainfall. After some 800 m, a horse trail comes in from the left, then, in another ten minutes, you come on the sign for the footpath to Teapot Hill on the right, a large garbage can beside it inviting you to dispose of discards on your return.

This path, well graded and easily ascended except for one series of steep stairs, soon brings you onto the summit ridge along which you walk to the south end where you are protected by cables from a steep drop-off. Here you enjoy the views across the lake to the ridge of Vedder Mountain and south along the Columbia Valley as it disappears into the blue south of the international border.

Before you leave the summit, you may notice a narrow trail from the east. This is the end of the other approach, a somewhat more sporting proposition than the one just described, which is so good that it may lack challenge since the whole trip takes little more than an hour.

For the alternative approach, travel Columbia Valley Highway for 5.4 km (3.4 mi) beyond Lakeside Lodge to a left fork on Frost Road at the sign for the Columbia Bible Camp. This road rises to a higher bench and splits at a T-junction where you go left on Watt Road for the camp. Here, drive round the sports field to the parking lot by the buildings and, as a courtesy, let the camp manager know that you are making for Teapot Hill.

The trail starts east of the dining hall and, after ignoring one left fork, you go left and descend into the valley of Watt Creek on what is actually the other end of Road 918. Having crossed the creek, take the left-hand fork, which gradually turns away from the stream. Continue along this road to cross another creek, about five minutes beyond which you come on a tree to the left with the figure seven incised in its trunk. Here, look for a narrow trail going off left. This is the lower end of the trail, which, at the top of the hill, you are told that you use at your own risk. It *is* steep, but in June it is adorned with honeysuckle and tiny starflowers, and really the only difficult spots may be a small washout near the summit and a little exposure here and there.

If the sound of this does not appeal, simply stay on the road for another 800 m and go up on the regular Parks Branch trail, returning by the same route.

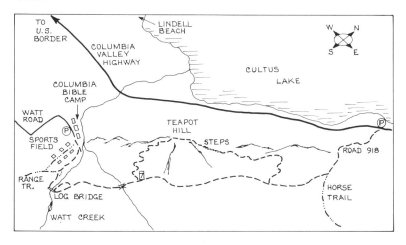

By Lindeman Lake

CHILLIWACK RIVER

80 LINDEMAN LAKE

Round trip 4 km (2.5 mi)
Allow 2 hours
High point 825 m (2700 ft)
Elevation gain 220 m (725 ft)
Trail
Best June to October

This reasonably short walk takes you up to one of the most beautiful lakes in the Chilliwack Valley region, a stretch of country that is now so popular for boating and fishing despite its distance from main centres of population. Actually, both the Parks and Outdoor Recreation Division and the Ministry of Forests now have campsites conveniently located for this and other outings near Chilliwack Lake, the new provincial park being at the northwest end of that fine body of water where the Chilliwack River emerges from it as a broad, fast-flowing stream. The Forest Service goes one better, having a small camping area right at the trail's beginning by Post Creek.

Going east on Highway 1, turn south at the Chilliwack-Sardis intersection and continue past the armed forces base to the Chilliwack River at Vedder Crossing. At the bridge go left on the road to Chilliwack Lake. This road crosses Post Creek 39 km (24 mi) up the valley, but the best parking for this hike is actually reached by going north (left) 0.5 km (0.3 mi) before this point, where a road leads you into the forest site by the creek and about 400 m upstream of the main road. Just on the east side of this bridge, the trail goes off upstream with the creek hurrying along on your left as you ascend. Actually this is part of the Centennial Trail but you would not know it, so active have the vandals been in removing signs; fortunately, the route is well trodden and clear so you should have no difficulty.

After some twenty minutes, you cross to the west bank, using a partly flattened log as a bridge. (Note: Another log, a little downstream, is also used but the approach to the higher one is better.) Now you climb steadily, the creek seeming to mock you as you toil upwards, a warm business on a sunny day, even if the pleasantly treed route does offer shade. This uphill pull continues for another fifteen minutes before you find the grade easing off, while the creek's impetuous rush changes to a gentle gliding motion. As you advance, you see great rocks that have tumbled from steep slopes, perhaps helping to dam up the valley and create the lake that is your objective.

Finally, you emerge from trees and there it is in front of you, confined in its narrow trough with craggy pinnacles rising from the ridge on the east, while the side you are on culminates in another ridge, invisible somewhere above you. Almost any spot along the banks will do for rest and rumination—plus a little fishing if your taste lies that way. As you look north along the steep slopes just above the water, you see the line of the Centennial Trail continuing, en route to Greendrop Lake and, eventually, to the Skagit Valley across the divide. You who are satisfied with the modest achievement of this goal, however, have the comfort of knowing that Lindeman is the more attractive; in fact, it has to rank high on any list of beautiful mountain lakes.

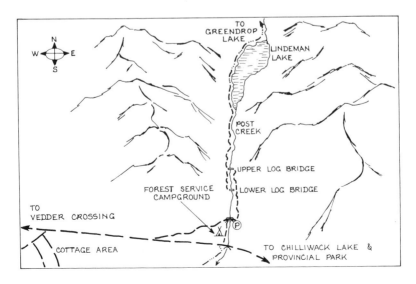

Logging bridge over the Chilliwack River

CHILLIWACK RIVER

81 LOWER POST CREEK

Round trip 4.8 km (3 mi)
Allow 2 hours
Forest trail
Good May to October

Like the hike to Lindeman Lake, this outing begins where the B.C. Centennial Trail crosses Chilliwack River Road 39 km (24 mi) east of the bridge at Vedder Crossing, a short distance west of the provincial park at the outlet end of Chilliwack Lake, and just before you cross Post Creek itself. There is parking for a few cars on the south side of the road, and here the trail descends the embankment heading towards the creek.

Though your route, identified by Centennial trail markers, parallels the course of the stream, you are sufficiently far from it on most of your walk to give your attention to the forest through which you are passing. This has quite large Douglas-firs and spindly lodgepole pines, the dense clumps of the latter contrasting with the relative isolation of the former. The active growth of lodgepole suggests these are replacements after forest fires; the fire-resistant cones of this tree open to deposit seeds after a conflagration, providing a striking instance of adaptability. Ground level, too, has its attractions, with the bunchberry flower in June carpeting either side of the path.

After about twenty-five minutes, if you are observant, you may notice a left fork to a ramshackle footbridge (minus handrails) over the creek. This is the old trail, which follows the east (left) bank to emerge on a logging road, with a short left turn bringing you to the bank of the Chilliwack River. However, a new section of the trail has been cleared as an alternative and this stays on the creek's west bank until you reach the logging road where a left turn leads you to the Post Creek bridge and, shortly thereafter, to the Chilliwack River crossing.

Note that the old trail did not make use of this bridge; it crossed a few yards downstream on what now looks like an extremely unsafe log, passage by which is not recommended except for those who wish to show off their prowess as tightrope walkers. Actually, the trail to the little picnic site by this log loops back to the Chilliwack River Bridge, and the open spot by the river is a pleasant spot for relaxing on warm days.

Your return may be by whichever trail you came out on; of course, though, you may make a loop of the latter part if you wish variety.

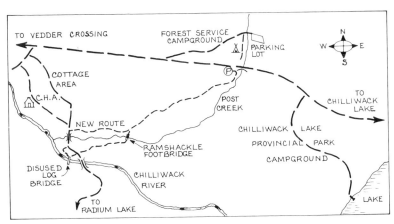

82 UPPER CHILLIWACK RIVER

Round trip (to shelter) 7.2 km
(4.5 mi)
Allow 3.5 hours
Trail
Good from late July to early October

Venturesome camper-hikers who have driven the rather rough 12.8 km (8 mi) of road south along Chilliwack Lake (sometimes closed for logging operations) find not one but two trails accessible to them: the route on the east bank gives access to the American side of the border; the other consists of a Forest Service track to Hanging Lake, the latter a full-day hike.

After you have driven the road, mainly single-track and somewhat potholey, you reach an attractive beach area just before the crossing of the upper river, and it is from a little east of this bridge that you set off upstream on the marked trail. This may occasionally be damp, especially in early summer, and you may find the lush vegetation something of a trial; the route, however, is well marked, being popular as part of a backpacking crossover to the Mount Baker area. Most striking are the treed sections, giant cedars, which leave you awed by their majesty but also saddened by the casualties among them, their roots undermined by the river in periods of high water. But the trees have another enemy: beaver. Here and there you come on trunks gnawed by these industrious engineers, even though they cannot rival man for destructiveness.

Thus you progress, crossing sloughs on footbridges or over the logs as you make for the Canada–U.S. border and your minor foray south of the

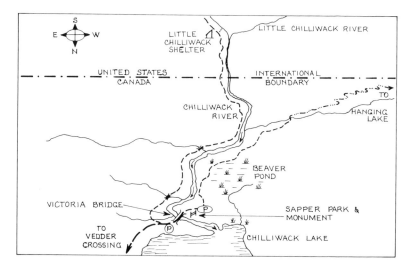

Upper Chilliwack River near Victoria Bridge

49th Parallel to the shelter hut. On your return, note the prolific growth of shrubs and flowers, including some exceedingly healthy devil's club. The open stretches give you glimpses of high peaks ahead, but, after the giant cedars, the river itself, in all its moods—now wave-capped and impetuous, now clear and placid—remains the chief attraction as you return to the bridge from which you set out.

This crossing, Victoria Bridge, gives access to what was originally the base camp set up by the British Royal Engineers when, in 1860, that corps was engaged in a survey of the boundary from which you have just returned. For this reason, the end of the lake has been set aside as Sapper Park, complete with commemorative monument. From this west side of the river the Hanging Lake trail heads off south, parallelling the river as it, like its neighbour, works its way through fine stands of cedar and past beaver ponds. It, however, strikes off west into a tributary valley, becoming rougher and steeper as it proceeds. If you do not wish a demanding hike, therefore, you should confine your stroll to the stretch along the valley floor, which itself gives you a respectable round trip of 3.2 km (2 mi).

Looking up the Skagit River

SILVER/SKAGIT

83 RHODODENDRON TRAIL (Skagit River)

Round trip 6.4 km (4 mi)
Allow 2 hours
High point 610 m (1950 ft)
Best in June and July

If, during the latter part of June, you are staying in the Provincial Silvertip Campground just west of where the road to Ross Lake crosses the Skagit River, you should not miss the chance to see the flowering of the red rhododendrons. These plants are not often seen in B.C., except under cultivation, though C. P. Lyons in his *Trees, Shrubs and Flowers to Know in British Columbia* does record their appearance along a 3-km (1.8-mi) stretch of Highway 3 some 11 km (6.8 mi) north of here. An additional source of interest connected with the trail you follow is its historic significance; it is, in fact, part of an old route to the interior of the province, the Whatcom Trail, created in 1858 for immigrants wishing to avoid the tax imposed by Governor Douglas on those entering via the Fraser River.

This walk in the Skagit Valley Recreation Area now appears to be free from the threat to raise the level of Ross Lake, so flooding the valley floor. To reach its beginning go south from Highway 1 a little west of Hope on to the Silver-Skagit Road. Travel nearly 43 km (27 mi) passing the campsite entrance a little before you cross to the east bank of the river. There, on the left, park in the recently created "26 Mile Bridge" picnic site and walk south along the road the short distance to the signposted trailhead.

Now on the track, you continue in open forest for some twenty-five minutes until you come on a foot trail at right angles to your line of travel. Before you turn off left on this, note the Centennial Trail marker to the right, for that route uses the old trail southwards. As you proceed north and east, heading back towards the river where it emerges from its deep valley, you join in imagination the illegal immigrants who used it long ago. Like them, you begin by wandering gently along on virtually flat terrain amid lodgepole pine, which gradually changes to more luxuriant growth while you descend from one old river terrace to another.

After some forty minutes you come on the first clusters of rhododendrons as you near the river, and the route lies among these colourful shrubs so long as you remain in the open valley. The farther you go, however, the more the trail rises and, since you are not making for the Hope-Princeton Highway, the bluff top where the gorge narrows dramatically makes a satisfying destination. From here you may feast your eyes on splendid views across to mountains such as Silvertip, as well as up and down the river. If you do not wish to go so far, you may make a short detour left just above the river to a large gravel bar where you may fish, sprawl, or glory in the view, always remaining conscious of the Skagit hurrying by.

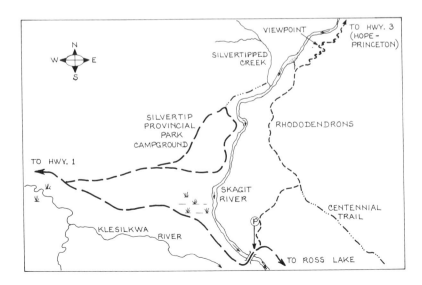

View across Ross Lake towards Redoubt Peak

SILVER/SKAGIT

84 SKYLINE TRAIL

Round trip 20 km (12.5 mi)
Allow all day
High point 1450 m (4700 ft)
Elevation gain 915 m (3000 ft)
Trail
Good June to September

Once again, as a walker rather than as a backpacker, you must content yourself with only a sampling of the section of the Centennial Trail that links the Skagit Valley with Manning Park, the complete crossover being beyond the scope of this book. What you do have on a day's outing are some breathtaking views of surrounding mountains, of the valley itself to where it opens out at the head of Ross Lake, and of all the innumerable flowers and shrubs that clothe the ridges in a rich mantle of colour in summer.

From the east side of the Silver-Skagit Road, 23.7 km (14.7 mi) south of the bridge spanning the Skagit River and 7.1 km (4.4 mi) north of the U.S. border, the trail begins, its entrance signposted. Note that limited parking exists across the road a short distance before the trailhead.

Once afoot, you strike into open forest; the trees are small but their shade gives pleasant walking out of the sun, and the occasional clearing provides the chance of seeing deer. After a few minutes, the main Centennial Trail from the north joins on the left, and shortly thereafter you cross a small creek—your last chance for water. After leaving this creek, you rise on a series of gravel benches, heading south and east, until after some forty minutes you come to one or two clearings and the first of your viewpoints. All along the way you should have been amply regaled by the flowers and shrubs, rein orchid, queen's cup, and bunchberry being prominent.

Still climbing steadily, you arrive after some ninety minutes at more views of Mount Hozameen to the southeast, with Redoubt Peak standing guard on the west side of the lake, and this point may be the destination for a round trip hike of 7.2 km (4.5 mi) lasting in all some three hours. If, however, you wish to make this walk a day's outing, you continue into the valley of a second creek before resuming the long climb to subalpine meadows. These provide an unforgettable sight in late July, with yellow aster, blue gentian, paintbrush, stonecrop, and many more all waiting to be admired.

This final destination is, of course, for strong walkers, but the rewards are commensurate with the energy expended. Even so, you see the trail still climbing up to the high ridges over which it travels to Gibson Pass in Manning Park.

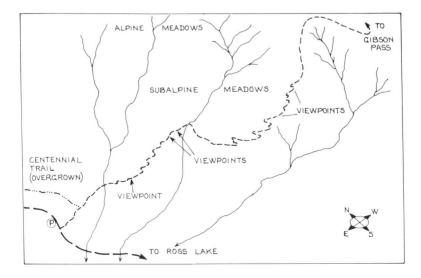

HOPE AREA

85 BRISTOL ISLAND AND PEBBLE BEACH

Bristol Island round trip 3 km (1.9 mi)
Allow 1 hour
Riverbank and road
Good, except during high water
Pebble Beach round trip 3.2 km (2 mi)
Allow 1.5 hours
Beach and old railway grade
Good, except during high water

If you are in the vicinity of Hope, here are two short walks, one on the south side of the Fraser, the other almost opposite on the north. One warning, though: They are possible only when the river level has dropped after runoff, something that may not happen till well into July, even in a normal year.

To take Bristol Island first, for it you leave Highway 1 at the Hope airport sign on Yale Road, almost directly opposite the indicator for Silver-Skagit Road. Continue north to cross the C.N. Railway track, having stayed right at the fork preceding it, then drive to just before the causeway that links the

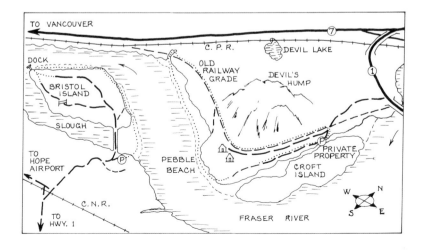

Booming ground from Bristol Island

"island" with the mainland. Turn right here and park, preparatory to dropping to river beach and your walk along the shoreline.

As you work round to the main river, you have Pebble Beach across the water from you, with Devil's Hump behind and Mount Ogilvie rearing its head skywards to the northeast. When walking downstream, you have one tricky stretch, the result of erosion, but once past this you may continue to the westernmost point, returning to your vehicle by a quiet country road amid fields and paddocks, the home of a number of riding horses.

For Pebble Beach, you drive north through Hope on Highway 1, cross the Fraser, and, a short distance beyond the bridge, turn sharp left on Landstrom Road. Follow it for about a kilometre, then fork left to park on a wide gravel stretch, dry much of the time but still serving to separate the public domain from Croft "Island" (private). From here, head west along the great pebble beds, your view opening up towards Silverhope Valley with its towering sentinel peaks.

Now you turn westwards downstream, gradually being forced towards the river's north bank by the thrust of its current until, a short distance below road and railway, further progress is barred by a tributary creek. From here, you may return as you came, but, if you wish, you may scramble up the bank to a disused railway grade and travel back along it, the steep slope of Devil's Hump on your left and the river screened from view by trees. Soon you see houses appearing below you on your right, and where railbed and road come close together, you descend to the latter for your short walk back to your car.

86 COQUIHALLA RIVER

Round trip from Coquihalla Road
9.6 km (6 mi)
Allow 3.5 hours
Elevation gain 375 m (1200 ft)
Best in June

This description provides two approaches to your walk's destination: the tunnels of the one-time Coquihalla Valley branch of the C.P.R. The former of these is the regular route, using the old railway grade itself; the longer and more adventurous takes you back in imagination to prerailroad days, for it lies along the old engineers' road to the Similkameen River.

For the railway approach, leave Highway 3 just under a kilometre east of its junction with Highway 1, turn left on Sixth Avenue at the Hope Golf Course sign, then go right on Kawkawa Lake Road. Cross the Coquihalla and drive to a fork at Hope Cemetery; stay right on Kettle Valley Road and continue to where three roads fork by an open space. Park here and proceed straight ahead on the old track, the swift-flowing river below you on your right. Though you do rise a little, the grade is not steep and you have plenty of time in spring to savour the balsam scent in the air as you walk along to the first tunnel for a round trip of 4.4 km (2.7 mi).

Stay left at the cemetery if you favour the alternative route, then, after Kawkawa Lake Road goes left, stay right on Othello Road. This is signposted as leading to Coquihalla Road and along it you drive 2.1 km (1.3 mi) before turning off right on a gravel road near a natural gas pumping station. Cross the pipeline right-of-way and park just beyond where a less-used track goes off right. Stay with this for some 200 m till you come to a giant Douglas-fir. Turn right again here and head uphill.

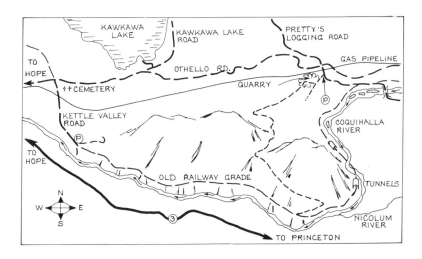

Old railway trestle over the Coquihalla River

Very soon, you again find yourself at an old road and on this you go left, following the Nicola Valley cattle trail that dates from 1878.

On this route you travel through attractive open forest, the sidehill being first on your right, then on your left as you turn to gain height. Next, you go between two hills and start descending, your track now heading to the left, following the Coquihalla Valley upstream. On this stage of your trip, open stretches give you a chance to admire the views, from the deep gorge of the river to the peak of Silvertip Mountain right ahead.

Thus you lose height, till just above the old railway right-of-way the trail doubles back and brings you down to it, some 800 m west of the tunnels. Walk to these, using a pocket torch if you have one to negotiate a rockfall in the first of them. Finally, you emerge on a small platform, beyond which further progress is impossible, a section of the trestle that spanned the canyon having been removed. The scene is awe-inspiring. Below is the river pent in its narrow gorge; straight across, one tunnel follows another, indicative of the difficulties faced by the pioneer railroad builders.

A faint track on your right as you emerge from the tunnel does lead down to a pebbly beach and you may wish to scramble down to appreciate the full grandeur of the scene. Back on the roadbed, you may wonder at the ingenuity used to push this line through such difficult terrain or picture to yourself, as you toil back up the trail towards the summit, the cattle drives that your route must have witnessed.

Note: Quarrying associated with the new Coquihalla Highway has, for the present, obliterated the northern approach to the cattle trail and made it hard to locate. You may, however, walk the quintette of tunnels, recently made accessible, by following the signs along Othello Road to park just by the river. It is hoped that the original route will be rehabilitated before long.

HOPE AREA

87 SPIRIT CAVE TRAIL

Round trip 7.2 km (4.5 mi)
Allow 3 hours
High point 610 m (2000 ft)
Elevation gain 520 m (1700 ft)
Trail
Good May to October

This walk, on a trail created by recipients of a 1973 summer employment grant, is not for the fainthearted or the ill-conditioned, rising as it does some 530 m (1700 ft) in less than 4 km (2.5 mi). However, the rewards, views along the Fraser Canyon, are more than compensation for the expenditure of energy if you go the whole distance; even if you make it only partway, you have ample recompense, both aesthetic and physical.

If you are travelling north on Highway 1 towards Yale, the trailhead is on the left of the road opposite a marker indicating the site of the old graveyard and just beyond a sign welcoming live visitors to the village. For a start, you travel upwards between two small creeks, finally swinging right and crossing one of them near the lower edge of a B.C. Hydro right-of-way. A little later, you cross a third creek, one that you will meet again higher up. Because the timber has been cleared off this area, you have a choice of striking vistas, upstream to Yale and beyond where the highway vanishes into a tunnel that pierces the prominent rock dome, Mount Lincoln, and below it the river feature, Lady Franklin Rock.

In spring, this trail is a naturalist's delight, when yarrow, wild strawberry, red-flower currant, bleeding heart, yellow violet, Oregon grape, and wild cherry all blossom and the balmy scent of cottonwood perfumes the air. As

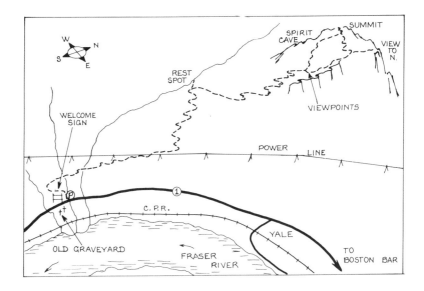

Routes to the coast, by river, rail and road

you rise above the power line, however, you enter open forest and climb steadily as various markers inform you. At 375 m (1200 ft) comes respite with a short side trail leading to a rest area by the creek where you may recruit your reserves of energy for what lies ahead.

What does remain is, first of all, a fairly level section along a steepish hill face, then come zigzags until the trail crests at just under 600 m (1950 ft) with an even more breathtaking view downriver, parallelled as the Fraser is by the highway and two railway tracks; even the power lines do not look too incongruous from this height in this picture of a major traffic artery created by natural forces and adapted by man for his own purposes. The eye, however, also catches the outlines of high mountains and ridges. Prominent among the latter is Zofka Ridge, named after the pioneer who prospected the Giant Mascot Mine near Hope.

Here you may be content to stop, but if you wish to continue, you have a choice: to follow the left-hand trail direct to the cave area or to continue along the edge to another viewpoint, this time of Silver Peak. From this spot, the trail cuts back left into the forest to a fork where a short jog right gives yet one more view, and the forward continuation takes you uphill to still another junction. Here the left-hand trail leads back via the cave to the main viewpoint and the way down, while the one to the right leads to a minor summit.

The caves themselves (there are actually more than one) consist of great hollows in shattered rock, but they are not particularly deep and after your surfeit of views are likely to be anticlimatic. Still, their situation does offer another outlook over the Coast and Lillooet mountain ranges and there is a solemn remoteness that is inspiring.

The Fraser River at Yale

HOPE AREA

88 HISTORIC YALE

Round trip 2 km (1.2 mi)
Allow 1 hour
Roads
Good all year

Next time you are driving north through Yale on the Fraser Canyon section of Highway 1, stop to read the message of the historical marker on the right of the road just south of the Canyon Inn Hotel. Better still, get out of your car for an hour or so and take a walk into the past; you will find plenty to interest you if you get away from the main road, saunter through the quiet streets of the old settlement, and look out on the river. Try to re-create the scene when this was a busy port, the Hudson's Bay Company fort dominating the landing area and freight wagons setting off northwards, not as today via a tunnel through a mountain but by a track that went up and over it.

Having parked close to the marker, drop downhill for one short block and turn left just before the C.P.R. tracks. Immediately behind the hotel you experience your first segment of history, the cairn commemorating the Cariboo Wagon Road, that feat of nineteenth-century civil engineering that opened up B.C.'s interior. Next, having passed the little railway depot, you come to the province's oldest church, the simple wooden Saint John's the Divine with its single small bell to call the faithful as it has done since 1860.

You are not yet finished with old churches, however, strange as it may seem in view of Yale's reputation for sin in gold rush days—or maybe because of it. Immediately after Saint John's, cross the railway tracks and, turning left again, continue your stroll northwards. In a small cluster of Indian houses just south of Yale Creek stands Saint Joseph's Roman Catholic Church, founded by the Oblate Father, Charles Grandidier OMI, in 1861, though the actual building is somewhat younger than its Anglican neighbour, dating as it does from 1880.

Returning through the village, go one block east of your outward route to follow the river on what was called, appropriately enough, Front Street, now peaceful and mainly deserted, with only a few of its buildings left and these by no means the originals. Standing on the bank by what was once a steamer landing, you look across the Fraser to the C.N.R. settlement and, if lucky, you may see one of its inhabitants cross the fast-flowing, turbulent waters in a small boat. In fact, if you are taking this walk in late summer when the river is low, you may drop down to the beach and extend your trip by wandering along it.

Note that here the Fraser is flowing roughly east and west, the start of its bend northwards being marked by a large rock in the midst of its channel. Lady Franklin Rock, as it is called, commemorates the visit to Yale in 1861 of the British polar explorer's widow. This landmark is in interesting juxtaposition with Mount Lincoln to the west of it, the latter name reflecting a strong American influence during gold rush days. Nowadays, though, its splendour is much diminished, pierced as it is by the highway tunnel and crowned with the local TV aerial on its summit. Thought of the tunnel, however, may remind you of the distance still to go; so, perforce, you turn uphill and recross the railway tracks back into the present.

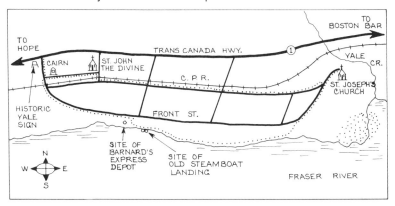

Deeks Creek

HOWE SOUND

89 DEEKS CREEK BLUFFS

Round trip 11.1 km (7 mi)
Allow 4 hours
High point 438 m (1400 ft)
Trail and taped route
Good May to October

This walk is for you only if you are experienced and feel venturesome, the trail being particularly steep at the start. The rewards, however, are a series of fine views across Howe Sound and, if you go far enough, along the valley of Deeks Creek.

For your starting point drive north on Highway 99 just over 16 km (10 mi) from the fork at Horseshoe Bay and park immediately beyond the creek (limited space). Your excitement begins with your dodging traffic as you cross the road and read the notice that this trail—the one-time route to Deeks Lake—has been superseded and that you use it at your own risk. If undeterred, you start climbing at once on the creek's west bank, your route marked with orange squares, and thus you proceed for some fifteen minutes to the first viewpoint.

Almost immediately beyond is the parting of the ways; the old hiking trail goes straight on while you fork left, following yellow markers and heading northwards. First you have another scramble to an open bluff, then in quick succession two or three more vantage points, any one of which may be a destination if you wish. Next comes some thirty-five minutes of forest walking before you reach two more lookout points, these being about 3.5 km (2 mi) from your start, and either being a possible destination. Note that by this time the yellow squares have given place to tapes.

If you decide to go beyond here, be careful to stay with the tapes as you travel in open forest or along disused logging roads. Finally, you break out into the open on such a road with a prominent rock bluff ahead. Go a little right, then left to ascend the steep track till, near the top, tapes direct you to the final viewpoint and its cairn. Here the outlook is specially striking and it is with a sense of accomplishment that you add your stone to the pile after having paid your respects to the scenery.

Note: From the same parking spot a new trail with orange markers, less steep and exposed than the old, begins some 120 m to the north of it and zigzags upward to meet the yellow trail after about 0.8 km (0.5 mi).

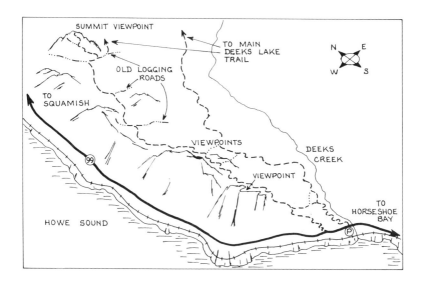

Goat's beard by the roadside

HOWE SOUND

90 MARION AND PHYLLIS LAKES

Round trip 16 km (10 mi)
Allow 5.5 hours
High point 530 m (1700 ft)
Elevation gain 470 m (1500 ft)
Logging roads
Good most of the year

A low-level trip on logging roads this; it is best undertaken, therefore, in winter or spring when the weather is still relatively cool, a bonus in the latter season being the wild flowers and shrubs along the route: queen's cup, bunchberry, fireweed, and false azalea to give a sampling. You have some interesting views, too, across Howe Sound and into the Vancouver watershed.

To reach this walk's beginning, turn sharp right off Highway 99 as you ascend the long hill after Furry Creek Bridge and 3.3 km (just over 2 mi) north of Porteau Provincial Park or 28 km (17.5 mi) beyond Horseshoe Bay. A gate just off the highway bars access to all but logging trucks, so your walk starts here.

For about forty minutes, you remain north of Furry Creek, having gone right at the first fork, where you stay with the lower road. The stream, when you cross it, is gentle in winter but presents a mad swirl of water following the spring run-off, its violence perhaps supporting the theory that "Furry" is a corruption of "Fury." Now you continue southeastwards, cross Phyllis Creek, and swing back west to gain height, this stretch giving you a fore-taste of the views across Howe Sound where Mount Sedgwick dominates the scene.

After resuming your original direction, you stay right at another fork just under a power line then stay parallel with it as, recrossing the creek en route, you traverse an area, logged a few years ago but now showing signs of renewed growth. Next comes Marion Lake, a possible destination, though its companion, Phyllis, is only some 400 m farther at the end of public access, the valley beyond the divide being within the Greater Vancouver Watershed District.

From here the great south shoulder of Mount Capilano rises eastwards on your left hand, and straight in front are the headwaters of the river whose name commemorates the North Vancouver Indians—the people of Kiap—and whose water supplies the people of the Lower Mainland.

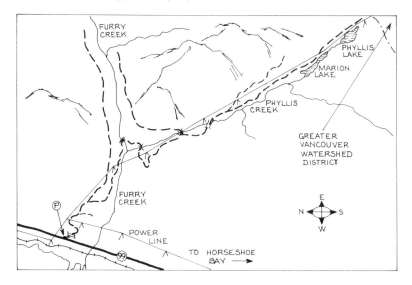

91 STAWAMUS SQUAW

Round trip 7.2 km (4.5 mi)
Allow 3 hours
High point 625 m (2000 ft)
Elevation gain 470 m (1500 ft)
Logging roads and trail
Best April to October

If, having looked at the statistics for hiking trails on the Chief massif, you have decided that these are beyond you, why not take this easy route to conquer his consort, thus enjoying views of Mount Garibaldi, of Mamquam with its great snowfields, even of the Chief, considerably less imposing from the summit you are now on. The drawback? Your approach via a MacMillan Bloedel logging road confines you to weekends and holidays.

After passing Shannon Falls Park a little south of Squamish Municipality, drive north for another 2.1 km (1.3 mi) to a right turn off Highway 99 a little before the bridge over Stawamus River. Travel 3.8 km (2.4 mi) to pick up the second of two roads leading uphill right, this after you have crossed the river (the watershed signs are apparently inoperative). On this road you drive, via a romantic gorge, to another crossing, with ample parking space just beyond. Actually, you may drive the short distance round the next bend if you wish; the road, however, is a little steep.

Above this bend, take the right fork, the less used road—last employed apparently for access to a tree thinning operation—and ascend in a series of long S bends, finally levelling off at about 500 m (1600 ft). After you have been on foot for about an hour, you come to a partly overgrown (at the time of writing) road on your right. Follow this road north towards your objective till, some fifteen minutes later, your route is joined from the left by the hiking trail from the Chief. You, however, stay right until, some 200 m beyond that junction, orange markers to your left direct you uphill on a well-graded

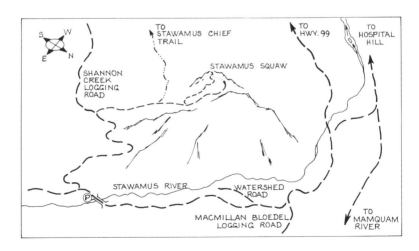

Looking towards Mamquam Mountain

footpath—once you have scrambled up the bank. Follow this track to the summit, working round the east side of the mountain in forest interspersed with cleared stretches.

Finally you arrive at the site of the one-time lookout tower, now dismantled, and it is from this location on the rocky knoll that you enjoy magnificent views in all directions. Your return is by the route already described, your eyes regaled, as you change direction, with a variety of scenes, including some interesting glimpses of the summit you have left behind you.

SQUAMISH/PEMBERTON

92 FOUR LAKES TRAIL

Round trip 5.6 km (3.5 mi)
Allow 2 hours
High point 290 m (950 ft)
Elevation gain 92 m (300 ft)
Trail
Good April to November

As in other areas administered by the Provincial Parks Branch, Alice Lake Park has a well-developed system of hiking trails. There are short ones like those round Alice Lake and Stump Lake, and long ones—Four Lakes Trail being the main example. This trail includes the paths already mentioned and adds to them the connecting links of a circuit involving Fawn Lake and Edith Lake, even though the latter is not, strictly speaking, in the park.

So well known is Alice Lake Park that it is scarcely necessary to say that you reach it by turning off Highway 99 some 9.7 km (6 mi) north of the turnoff for Squamish town centre and driving to one of the parking lots, preferably the one just east of the sani-station, which is reached by staying left and driving uphill at the park entrance instead of making for the lake. Here, in an open space north of the road and just beyond the right turnoff into the campsite location, you have the pointer for Stump Lake Trail to your left, and from it you start your walk.

At first you are in thick bush, but this thins out when you reach the fork where the arms of the Stump Lake circuit separate, leaving you free to choose whichever you wish. The right arm gives views over DeBeck Hill and towards the Tantalus Range; from the left arm you see Mount Garibaldi and Alice Ridge; each gives glimpses of the lake and its clusters of water lilies. At the far end, beyond a little island, the trails join and here you fork right again.

Back in deep forest, you become aware of the increased rush of water and soon you find yourself just above the Cheekye River, which flows down from Mount Garibaldi, its valley separating Brohm Ridge and Alice Ridge.

On this stretch the influence of the stream is manifest in the near rain-forest effect that is produced, quite a bit different from the vegetation elsewhere. The difference soon becomes obvious as you climb steadily eastwards, rising to the trail's high point as you near Fawn Lake; lush skunk cabbage gives way to salal, and alder to miniature conifers.

Fawn Lake is a little off the trail to the right. Where the spur road goes off to it, the foot trail you have been on develops into a logging road, a status it is to maintain till you reach lake number three, Edith Lake.

En route, when you come to a major intersection, the route crossing yours is the main approach to Alice (Cheekye) Ridge, an approach that antedated creation of the park so that it must remain in being because it gives access to the forest lands above.

At this lake, go right at the first turnoff, then right again, leaving the logging road for a footpath as a prelude to your descent to Alice Lake on the last stretch. For a good part of this section, the trail jostles lush vegetation, and finally path and watercourse together arrive at the south end of the lake. From here you may use either shore to return to your transport. Each is pleasant, but perhaps the one on the east side is the prettier, having views of DeBeck Hill across the water; it is also a little shorter.

At the north end you must return to pavement again, but only for a short distance as you walk up through the campsites to the intersection with the park headquarters road where your car is parked.

This low-level walk on well-made trails, carefully signposted, is good for those times of the year when more ambitious outings are out of reach because of weather. The only difficulty is that individuals vandalize the signs, tearing some of them down or reversing them so that they are not always completely accurate; on the whole, though, common sense indicates which way to go despite such antisocial activity.

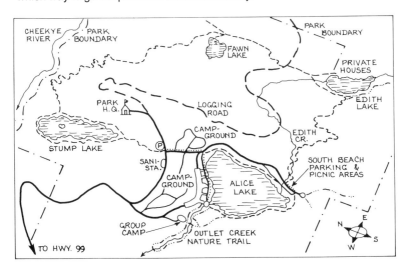

93 DeBECK HILL

Round trip 4 km (2.5 mi)
Allow 1.5 hours
High point 420 m (1350 ft)
Elevation gain 200 m (640 ft)
Old logging road
Good April to November

Though the upper part of the route to this miniature mountain has suffered from the construction of a CBC television repeater tower, this trip is still very much worthwhile, if only for the tremendous panorama from its summit. And not all is lost, either; the lower part of the original logging road you use is very much as it always was, even to the mellowing signs of past activity: rusted cable, an old power winch abandoned and forlorn, and what is left of a sawdust pile.

The start of your hike is the South Beach parking lot in Alice Lake Park, from which you walk south via the turnaround for cars and make your way over, under, or around the barrier that blocks off the maintenance yard, ignoring the signed trail to Easter Seal Camp, which goes off left. Just inside the yard on your right as you enter it, the one-time logging road angles back uphill to an old quarry. Here, you may be at a loss for a moment or so as the track seems to vanish; however, if you look left, you see it continuing gently southwestwards from beside a pile of loose sand.

After some twenty minutes, take the right fork uphill where the route splits, and now you find yourself travelling north below some impressive bluffs above you on your left. It is on this stretch that you come on signs of bygone logging and, unfortunately, some recent bulldozing, the aftermath of construction. One can only hope that nature will soon reassert itself. Beyond here, you swing back left and continue in a southerly direction to the next sharp turn that takes you back right again. From here a walk of another 200 m or so takes you to the summit, where, having tuned out the TV monstros-

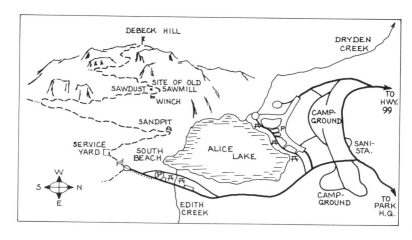

Southeast towards Mount Habrich

ity, you can forget the works of man and enjoy the beauties of nature: the great peaks and glaciers of the Tantalus Range on the west side of the Squamish River Valley and the impressive summits of Mount Garibaldi above you on the east. And the nearer scene has its charms as well: the park, densely treed, below you on the right; the Cheakamus Valley stretching north with Cloudburst Mountain to the left of it; and, in the southwest, flat delta lands around Squamish at the head of Howe Sound.

Levette Lake and Alpha Mountain

SQUAMISH/PEMBERTON

94 LEVETTE AND HUT LAKES

**Round trip (Levette Lake) 5.6 km
(3.5 mi)
Allow 3 hours
High point 425 m (1400 ft)
Elevation gain 245 m (800 ft)**

**Round trip (Hut Lake) 13 km (8 mi)
Allow 5 hours
High point 625 m (2000 ft)
Elevation gain 405 m (1300 ft)
Disused logging roads
Good May to October**

Actually this walk can give you three lakes rather than two, Evans Lake providing a short outing in contrast to the time and exertion required for the other two. The longer trip, though, has ample compensation, since the mountain views as you travel add to the pleasure.

To reach your starting point, drive on Highway 99 north from Squamish to the Alice Lake Park junction. Here turn left and downhill for Cheekye, bear right, crossing the BCR tracks, and cross the Cheakamus River at Fergie's Fishing Lodge. Turn right immediately on Paradise Valley Road and drive for 2.1 km (1.3 mi) to a left turn opposite North Vancouver Outdoor School.

Follow this road uphill for 1.3 km (0.8 mi) to a junction, where a left fork (private) leads to Evans Lake Forest Camp. The right-hand road is your route.

From here, the old logging road is too rough for ordinary cars so, having parked, you set off in deep second-growth forest, your first point of note being the turnoff left to the public access area of Evans Lake, to which the return trip takes about thirty minutes. As you press on northwards, you start rising and the trees thin out, still giving some shade on a hot day, however, while allowing you glimpses back towards the Sky Pilot summits thrusting themselves skywards.

After about forty-five minutes of walking, you stay right where the road forks, a procedure that you repeat a few minutes later where a road marked "Private" leads to cabins. For Levette Lake, you go left some ten minutes later, soon to arrive at a little bluff above this picturesque body of water in its rock basin. Here you stop, surrounded by tall Douglas-firs, with, as a magnificent backdrop, the peaks, snowfields, and glaciers of the Tantalus Range.

For Hut Lake (also called Hud), you stay right at the fork just mentioned and start rising steadily to not quite 625 m (2000 ft). En route, one more viewpoint gives an excuse for you to rest and feast your eyes before resuming your ascent to the col. Once beyond, you pass a dark little reedy pond on your left, then, as your trail swings west before descending into the lake basin, you come on another viewpoint—and possible destination if you are no aficionado of lakes—on a small bluff just to the right with the whole valley of the Squamish River far below and Mount Tantalus itself towering above, the round trip to here being 9.6 km (6 mi).

If you do continue, you arrive suddenly and unexpectedly at the pretty little Hut Lake, the only trouble being the need to regain height on your return. Actually, this would make a pleasant overnight backpack trip, leaving the ascent for the following morning.

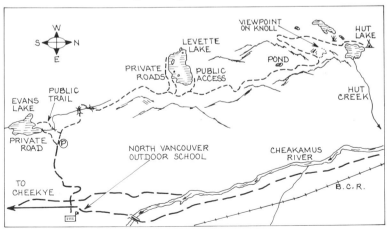

The Black Tusk from near the trapper's cabin

SQUAMISH/PEMBERTON

95 TRICOUNI TRAIL

Round trip (from river) 9.6 km (6 mi)
Allow 4 hours
High point 700 m (2300 ft)
Elevation gain 400 m (1300 ft)
Road and trail
Good June to October

Your route for this walk is one created by climbers making for the alpine country on the divide between the valleys of the Cheakamus and Squamish, hence its unofficial title. Obviously the climbers' objective lies far beyond the scope of an outing suitable for this book; however, a little lake—unnamed on maps of the area, though locally known by such titles as Gilders, Trapper's or Cedar—does provide a satisfying turnabout point.

Going north on Highway 99 some 21 km (13.1 mi) beyond the turnoff to Alice Lake Park and shortly after the road has levelled off following its descent to the Cheakamus River, go left at the road signposted to the one-time Alpine Lodge and park just before the bridge. In case you do miss the turn, note that it is 1.5 km (0.9 mi) south of the sign for the Black Tusk parking area.

Since the construction of a logging road the old trail has deteriorated and become so overgrown that it is no longer easily followed. Besides, the approach crosses private property and is now out of bounds. However, the logging road provides an acceptable substitute for weekends or holidays when it is free of heavy truck traffic.

To follow this route, cross the river and the B.C. Railway tracks, then turn left and head downstream until the road turns right and uphill. One advantage of the new route, you will find as you traverse the hillside, is the view over Lucille Lake towards the Barrier on the opposite side of the valley. Another feature of interest a short distance beyond is the devil's brickyard of shattered columnar basalt.

Next comes a gate just before a fork where you take the right-hand road and about a kilometre farther on you reach a cleared area with striking views over the upper Cheakamus towards the Black Tusk. Just on the far margin of the forest look on your left for the trail, marked with an orange square and three horizontal lines.

From here to the trapper's cabin by the lakes takes only a few minutes and, staying left where the climbers' route forks right, you may ascend the rounded bluff behind the hut for more fine vistas to the south and east.

Note: The beginning of the walk passes through private property. Please respect the owners' privacy and stay on the road.

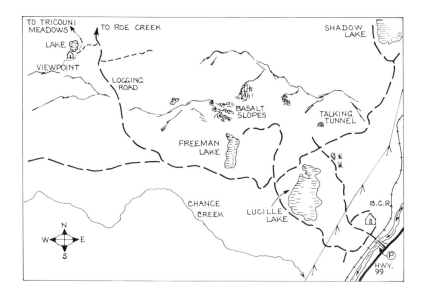

SQUAMISH/PEMBERTON

96 BRANDYWINE FALLS PARK

Round trip 4 km (2.5 mi)
Allow 1.5 hours
Old logging road and trails
Good May to October

Though this scenic area has been designated as a day-use park for a number of years, the Parks Branch has so far carried out only minimal improvements at the one-time resort so that many pass by on their way to Alta Lake unaware of what they are missing: the waters of the creek rushing headlong over a great basalt sill into the cauldron below, where the spray-cloud resembles steam rising from the depths.

Not long after you have passed Daisy Lake as you travel north on Highway 99, you cross the B.C. Railway from right to left and, immediately after, you become aware of an open space on the right, adorned with two A-frames, two chemical toilets, and some litter barrels. Park in this area. At the far end, a road with a locked gate leads to a crossing of the creek. Next it crosses the railway, and a footpath to the falls viewpoint branches off right a little beyond.

But the view from above is only part of the attraction. If you do not mind a descent of some 95 m (300 ft), you may make the north end of Daisy Lake your destination by staying with the old road at the viewpoint fork. This track leads downwards, veering south in the process, amid some interesting basaltic rock formations, silent witness to the igneous activity that helped create the falls. At length, having perhaps done a little boulder-hopping at one of the creek's outflow channels, you reach the lakeside with its driftwood and mixed grasses—that is, providing it is not the season of high water when that goal would be out of reach across a rushing flood.

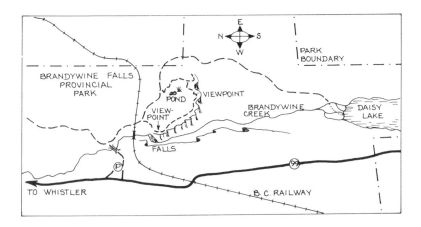

Brandywine Falls

To your right is the main course of Brandywine Creek, a possible fishing spot for anglers. For others there is the peace of the place, contrasting with the violence above. Don't forget, though, when you embark on this little side trip, that your return trip is uphill.

Aerial tram over Cheakamus River

SQUAMISH/PEMBERTON

97 CHEAKAMUS LAKE

Round trip 6.4 km (4 mi)
Allow 3 hours
High point 840 m (2725 ft)
Park trail
Good late June to October

This fine body of water, just 3.2 km (2 mi) inside the western boundary of Garibaldi Provincial Park, provides a variety of picturesque spots along its north shore, with views across the lake to the McBride Range and the glaciers of the park's high country. Two cautions, though: The approach road has been receiving only minimal attention and can be rough in spots; snow, too, can lie long in this country, so save this hike for high summer or fall.

The approach road (signposted) turns off to the right from Highway 99 just beyond Alta Lake Municipal Hall if you have travelled the 45 km (28 mi) north from the Alice Lake turnoff, and 0.5 km (0.3 mi) beyond the B.C. Railway crossing that rejoices in the unofficial title of Function Junction. The gravel road you are now on passes a works yard, then forks. Here you go left, again following the sign, and begin to rise a little while traversing a logged-off stretch of country that is just beginning to come back. At 3.2 km (2 mi) you fork left again, climbing steadily towards the road's end at a small parking area with its register for hikers and wilderness campers.

From here, the trail heads east, crossing two small creeks before bringing you to the park boundary. Now you continue eastwards in tall timber, an indication of what this whole area must have been like before so much of it was logged. Progress is easy, for the trail remains virtually level as it gradually converges with the Cheakamus River. After some thirty minutes, you come on a sign pointing right for Helm Lake Trail, one of the routes into the high country to the south; it is worth making this short side trip to the river crossing to view the human-powered aerial tramway, an interesting method of transportation, though somewhat hard on arms and hands, particularly for parties of three or fewer.

On rejoining your trail, continue through the forest with its healthy growth of devil's club, especially where the route is close to the riverbank. Gradually you notice the current slackening, the water becomes a deeper green, and vistas of the lake begin to open out ahead of you until you find yourself at its western end.

Any spot along the shore may serve as a destination. The trail itself continues for some way along the lake's north side, growing gradually fainter the farther you go. On this stretch, the alternation of treed areas with avalanche-created open spaces gives nice contrasts in vegetation, the clear forest floor being interspersed with stretches of lush grass and flowers where the sun exerts its power. There is, too, a rocky face above some dark-looking water that may require some care to negotiate.

Wherever you do stop, you have rewarding views; in addition, fishing is a possibility if you have come prepared. You are not disturbed by noisy powerboats either; there aren't any, and one can only hope that the peace will be allowed to continue, especially if plans go ahead to extend the trail towards Singing Pass.

Return poses no problems either. It is pleasant to wander along the trail through the forest until the trees thin out at the park boundary. Across the river, too, an interesting lava flow shows itself and farther away to the west rises Metaldome Mountain, with Mount Sproatt on its right. Even the threat of a rough approach road should not deter you from this satisfying outdoor experience.

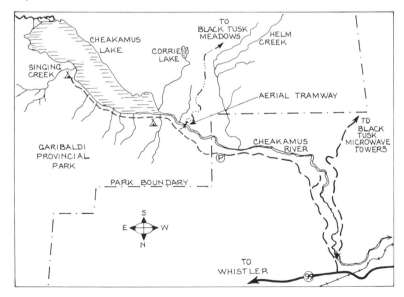

View up Fitzsimmons Creek, Blackcomb Mountain on left

SQUAMISH/PEMBERTON

98 RAINBOW FALLS

Round trip 3.2 km (2 mi)
Allow 1 hour
High point 820 m (2700 ft)
Elevation gain 152 m (500 ft)
Good May to October

If you are staying at Whistler and have a spare hour some evening before dinner, try this short walk as an aperitif.

To reach the start of this outing, take the road that branches west off Highway 99 about 1.2 km (0.7 mi) south of the Whistler Mountain parking lot, or 1.6 km (1 mi) north of the B.C. Railway crossing. First you pass some barracklike condominiums before crossing the B.C. Railway track, then, after little Nita Lake, you come to the main lake with its youth hostel sign. Continue for 1.6 km (1 mi) beyond the hostel, passing the old Rainbow Station on your right and, finally, just where the road crosses the creek, park on its south bank to the left.

The signposted trail, its beginning marked with tape, ascends the bank on the left where the road has been cut through the natural slope of the hill. The grade, however, soon evens off, and you find yourself ascending parallel with the course of the stream, among second growth for a start, but later among tall shade-giving trees. The rush of water below you on the right is all that breaks the stillness until, after some fifteen minutes, you find your track converging with the creek and you come upon the lower falls, set in a cool and shady valley.

Continue a short distance farther upstream to emerge at the foot of the upper falls where the creek plunges over a rock sill into a fine pool before regaining momentum for its next dash. On this last stretch, you will have noticed the Rainbow Lake trail angling uphill to the left; if you want a little more exercise, you may retrace your steps a short distance and ascend it once you have enjoyed your view of the falls. This track rises 62 m (200 ft) out of the ravine towards a logged-over stretch, finally converging with an old, somewhat eroded logging road from which views open out dramatically.

Ahead, and a little to the right, other rapids and falls stretch some distance upstream on the creek and behind and above rises a shoulder of Rainbow Mountain. More spectacular, though, is the prospect across the valley to the east. Spread out before you is Green Lake, aptly named when you see the shimmer of its glacial water; behind it are the glaciers of Wedge Mountain and Weart Mountain shining in the evening sun, rendering Whistler Mountain to the southwest somewhat puny by contrast. Between these two areas of high country lies the deep valley of Fitzsimmons Creek, with the mountain country round its head just visible in the distance.

Now comes return down the trail and back to the road. If you want to turn this into a longer walk, however, you may continue on the old road till it splits a little farther up the hill, with the left branch heading south a short distance along the lower slopes of Mount Sproatt. From here views open out even more, so your extra effort is amply rewarded.

As for the right fork, it supplies hikers and climbers with access to the alpine country around Sproatt and Rainbow, country that contains two small lakes named—believe it or not—Gin and Tonic, as well as Rainbow Lake itself.

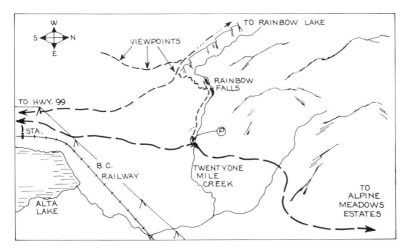

99 LOST LAKE CIRCUIT (Whistler)

Round trip 7.2 km (4.5 mi)
Allow 2.5 hours
Trail and old logging road
Good June to October

What do you do at Whistler in summer? Well, you may enjoy a walk around Lost Lake, now a municipal park, combining your outing with a swim on a warm day and filling your eyes with the beauties of Blackcomb Mountain, Singing Pass, and Whistler to the east, with Rainbow and Mount Brew to the west and south.

Drive north on Highway 99 to Whistler Village, 5.1 km (3.2 mi) beyond the Rainbow Lake turnoff. Go off right a little before the school, then turn left on Village Gate Boulevard and pass the R.C.M.P. office before parking at the north end of Lot 3, close to the signpost pointing to Lost Lake Park. Once on foot, proceed along an avenue of trees, arriving at an open space just above the confluence of Fitzsimmons and Blackcomb creeks. Here, cross the two bridges, so staying on the left-hand trail to your objective. Remain on this trail for a kilometre, passing one or two interesting beaver dams en route and ignoring tracks to the left. Now, at a major fork, cross the lake's outlet creek to the right and continue east to its bathing beach and a possible dip.

To proceed counterclockwise, continue on an old logging road that stays fairly close to the shoreline, giving you varied glimpses south across the water until, at the lake's northwestern end, you fork left on Westside Trail. At

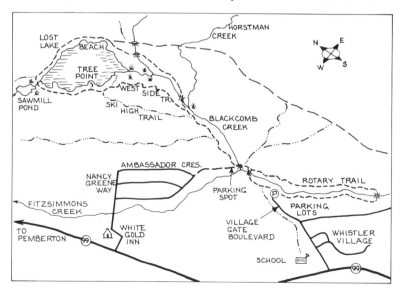

Lost Lake

first, you may think this something of a disappointment because of the belt of trees separating you from the water; however, by taking a small track left, you find yourself on Tree Point, the views from which more than make up for any deprivation. From here, looking across to the swimming area, you have the whole of the valley's eastern side, its peaks and passes, before you.

Resuming your walk, you again reach the bridge at the outlet for return to the meeting of the creeks. To prolong the outing, and the pleasure, however, do not cross Fitzsimmons; instead, stay left and pick up Rotary Trail as it follows the creek upstream on its north bank to a footbridge. Here, a turn to the right and a walk downstream on the opposite side brings you back to your point of departure.

Top of the upper Nairn Falls

SQUAMISH/PEMBERTON

100 NAIRN FALLS

Round trip 5 km (3 mi)
Allow 2 hours
Park trails
Good May to November

Because of their distance from Vancouver—they lie a little south of Pemberton and 32 km (20 mi) north of Mount Whistler—these falls are perhaps not as well known as they ought to be. That may be all to the good, however; viewpoints are limited, and the warning at the beginning of the trail is not to be taken lightly since a slip on the rocks could be serious. Indeed, the appropriate adjective from this sample of the unleashed power of nature is "sublime" in its original sense of "inspiring admiration and terror," and few visitors return from a visit to the falls with senses unstirred.

To reach the start of the trail, turn sharp off the highway at the Nairn Falls Park sign and drive into the camping area for about 300 m, staying right at each intersection. The trail sign itself is on the right just by a campsite, so park as close to it as possible without blocking access. Note also that dogs are to be kept on leash, a necessary precaution in view of the narrow trail's proximity to the river.

From its start at a viewpoint about 22 m (70 ft) above the water where the Green River makes a turn to the east, the trail heads south, gradually approaching the water till after about 800 m it is just above the current and separated from it by only a narrow beach. Along the way, tall conifers provide shade, welcome in summer, as the route begins to rise to the ever-louder rush of falling water. After crossing a narrow footbridge, you emerge finally on a platform of water-smoothed rock with its dramatic view of the upper fall where the river launches itself headlong into a narrow abyss amid a cloud of boiling spray. Just as spectacular is the way it turns at right angles to its original course to get round the rock barrier in its path before going over the lower fall.

This latter is more difficult to see clearly, its full majesty being visible only from a rocky outcrop to which you must descend as best you can, with the necessity of getting back up again. To continue farther along the trail is difficult, too, as you have to scramble for a short distance to reach an upper level space. And after this excitement comes anticlimax because once you have scrambled to the top of the falls, all you see is a mountain stream hurrying on its way with little hint of the drama below.

Besides the falls, their setting is worth a word. To the east Mount Currie rises above a wild wooded gorge, while to the south are the steep slopes from which the right-of-way of both road and railway have had to be carved. Indeed, sight of a B.C. Railway freight crawling uphill is quite dramatic as a contrast to the onward rush of the river.

Don't hurry this trip. Besides using the falls trail, sample the other paths in the park that stretch along the river lower down, where it resumes its north-ward journey to mingle its waters with the Lillooet River below Pemberton.

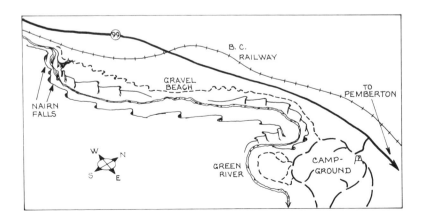

217

Ladder on Soames Hill

SECHELT

101 SOAMES HILL

Round trip 3.2 km (2 mi)
Allow 1.5 hours
High point 280 m (900 ft)
Elevation gain 185 m (600 ft)
Trail
Good much of the year

As you approach Langdale by B.C. ferry from Horseshoe Bay, you are conscious if you remain on the boat deck instead of joining the stampede for cars of what Dr. Samuel Johnson would have called a considerable protuberance, right on the coast and a short distance south of the ferry dock. This is the 275-m (900-ft) Soames Hill, known locally as "The Knob," the summits of which provide various views: south along the Sunshine Coast to Shoal Channel and Keats Island, west to Sechelt Ridge and Mount Elphinstone, and east over the island-dotted waters of Howe Sound to the mountain chain along its eastern shoreline.

One beginning for this hike, at present, comes at the top of a rise on the right of Marine Drive (stay left at the North Road fork if you are coming from the ferry) about 1.6 km (1 mi) south of the Langdale terminal traffic light. Here, limited parking is available where an old road angles uphill and opposite a nest of mail delivery boxes (note that a possible housing development may lead to changes). Walk up this track but stay left at a fork just before a quarry. Now you are on a path working your way southwest round the flank of the hill and running into forest before you start your steep ascent, the improved trail using flights of steps to ease the gradient on steeper sections.

After you have struggled up the final ladder, note your return route, which goes more or less straight ahead; you, however, veer to the right and continue upwards on the south edge of the trees, the view over Gibsons (once Gibson's Landing, hence the final "s") opening out as you progress. Finally, on the main (south) summit your outlook expands to include the Sechelt coast round to Gower Point as well as the islands, and here you may wish to enjoy your success. Don't go near the edge, however, for the bluffs are steep.

The north summit behind you is tree-clad and offers no comparable views, so, returning to your fork at the top of the ladder, turn right for a sight of Mount Elphinstone and the islands up Howe Sound before heading left for the trail that offers an alternative descending route.

This track takes you west, but you have yet another viewpoint to the south and west before you start down on a series of long ladders, the risers furnished with handrails. At the foot, you find yourself in a small clearing with, in addition to your foot trail left, an old road coming in through trees from the west. This road provides an alternative approach from Bridgeman Road, reached from Chamberlin Road, which itself forks from North Road 2.7 km (1.7 mi) from the Langdale ferry exit, but is unmarked at present.

To use this alternative for an ascent, park where Bridgeman swings left and becomes Boyle, opposite an old road among trees (the other end of the one you see in the clearing). Follow this into the bush for 500 m to reach this spot. Now, as you follow the trail east round the base of the hill for a return to Marine Drive, you see yet another trail coming from the right to join yours. This has originated on Chamberlin also, but some 600 m downhill from the Bridgeman turnoff. Its only advantage is to provide a choice of an east or west approach, depending on whether you turn left or right.

If the subdivision on Marine Drive does go ahead, it may be that access will be limited to the latter two approaches; perhaps, though, the builder will be public-spirited and leave an easement to this scenic miniature mountain with its arbutus, conifers, and dogwood, and its marine and mountain views.

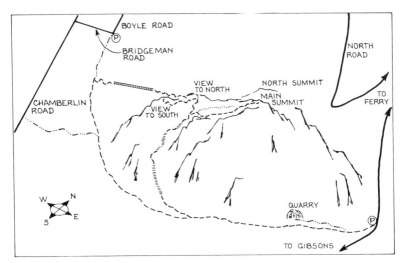

SECHELT

102 CABLE TRAIL

Round trip 7.2 km (4.4 mi)
Allow 3.5 hours
High point 945 m (3100 ft)
Elevation gain 735 m (2400 ft)
Trail and logging road
Best June to October

This walk is not for you if you want to get fit; only if you *are* fit should you set out on the trail as it rises from 214 m (700 ft) to 975 m (3200 ft) in little more than 3.5 km (2.2 mi). On the other hand, it does give you some nice open forest for a warm day, followed by a ridge with extensive views south, west, and east.

To reach the trail's beginning, travel west from the Langdale ferry terminal, staying right at the North Road–Marine Drive fork then turning right

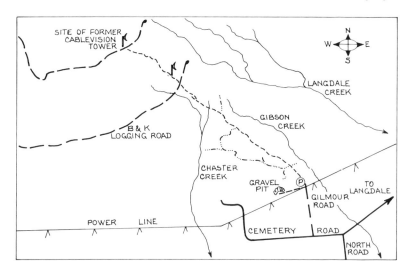

View from upper station

again after almost 4 km (2.5 mi) on Cemetery Road, with yet another right fork when you reach Gilmour Road. Drive to the end of this road just beyond the power line by a small cable television relay hut on the edge of forest and before some buildings. Park clear of the road.

Once embarked, your rule at all intersections is to choose the trail that follows the cable line as it rises through impressively old second-growth forest with, occasionally, the sound of Gibson Creek below you and to your right. At first, the ground vegetation on either hand is moss, but this gradually gives way to blueberry bushes as you leave the forest for a recently logged stretch. Next you cross a logging road—the B & K that leaves Highway 101 by Cliff Gilker Park—and shortly thereafter you reach the lower receiver station, with its rather limited outlook, 2.8 km (1.7 mi) from your start point.

You are now on the main south ridge of Mount Elphinstone as, after regaining your breath, you continue upwards, still following your friendly cable to its upper terminal on a trail that is now steep and open so that you may use the view as an excuse for a short breather. In season, too, you may want to admire the massed bunchberry in flower, interspersed as it is with lily of the valley. At the top station you have every incentive to sit and gaze over the Strait of Georgia and the islands at the mouth of Howe Sound: Bowen, Keats, and Pasley being especially prominent. Eastwards across the sound you have the impressive peaks, such as Harvey and Brunswick, that rise from its waters, while above you looms Mount Elphinstone itself.

Note: The cable and the towers have been dismantled; however, enough of the cable is left for you to follow should you be in doubt.

103 CLIFF GILKER PARK

Round trip 4 km (2.5 mi)
Allow 1.5 hours
Forest trails
Good all year

The one-time Sunshine Coast Recreation Centre has now acquired a name of its own and is classed as a park, an indication, presumably, that plans for a recreation complex on the site have been shelved or abandoned. As it now exists, however, it has a beauty of its own and its trails provide an ideal introduction to forest walks, with two scenic creeks added for good measure. Nor does it lack recreational facilities: besides picnic tables here and there, it contains a children's adventure playground.

The park is located just to the right of Highway 101 approximately 9.5 km (6 mi) beyond the supermarket shopping centre in Gibsons as you travel west; it is just east of a golf course as well. At the sign, a road goes off uphill and a short distance in you come on a large directional sign showing trails and parking areas, one of them located just beyond, at a point where a trail goes off right into the forest. The longest circuit involves a crossing of both Clack Creek and Roberts Creek, as well as the old B & K logging road.

For this outing, you may proceed counterclockwise, downstream on Clack Creek from just above Basalt Gorge and proceeding to its bridge over Shadow Falls. Cross here and continue on the right-hand trail to cross Roberts Creek as well, staying right once more at the next fork and traversing the logging road already mentioned. This stretch of your walk is in beautiful forest, a state of affairs that continues after you have recrossed the road for return to an upstream crossing of Roberts Creek at a natural

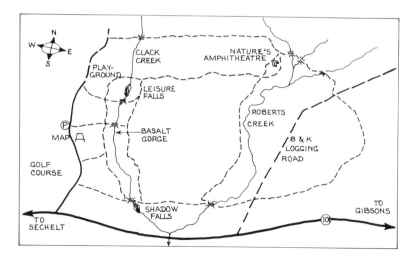

Clack Creek

amphitheatre. Continue upstream on the left of the current until your route veers left and, after making your way over Clack Creek, you catch a glimpse of the golf course to your right as you swing south. Next comes the playground and you go left here into the forest again at yet another waterfall. From it, you may return down either bank of the stream.

For a shorter circle, begin as described but take the left bank trail upstream at Roberts until you hit a path veering left. This brings you to Clack Creek above its upper falls and a choice of either bank for your return to the middle bridge, making a round trip of 2.4 km (1.5 mi).

Log bridge high above Chapman Creek

SECHELT

104 CHAPMAN CREEK FALLS

Round trip 4.5 km (2.8 mi)
Allow 2 hours
Service road and trail
Good most of the year

This creek, a healthy stream almost approaching the status of a river, is the source of the water supply for the municipality of Sechelt so you should be particularly careful to avoid polluting it as you travel to the top of its falls.

Access is from Highway 101, 1.8 km (1.1 mi) east of the Sechelt four-way stop light where you go uphill on Selma Park Road for some 350 m then turn sharp left on a dirt road and continue upwards to meet a power line right-of-way at the top of the rise above the little town. Here you are just west of a fenced-off reservoir and you stay to the west of it as you start along the pipeline road into the bush.

As with the walk to Crowston Lake, you may leave your vehicle at any suitable point from the power line on, the longest walk from the edge of the forest giving you no more than a round trip of 4.5 km (2.8 mi) on what is usually a fairly peaceful service road. As you travel through dense second-growth forest, you become gradually more aware of the sound of rushing waters and then finally comes your first view of the falls: an awe-inspiring sight.

Here the road ends and the large pipe appears from under its surface. Now you proceed along a duckwalk to the catchment area just by the upper fall where there are numerous vantage points from which to view the cascading waters.

Should your taste lie in the direction of a forest trail by the creek in a somewhat gentler mood, however, you may indulge that also by following the power line road east from the reservoir some 500 m, then going left to park in an open space beyond which a marked trail leads into the forest. From here you can travel upstream on a trail that descends gradually to the creek and finally peters out by a deep pool; a favoured fishing spot for local anglers.

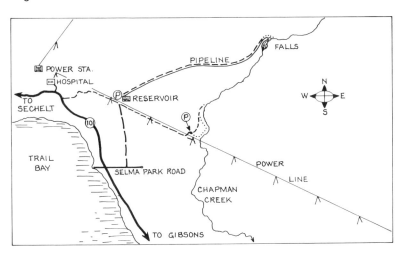

105 CROWSTON LAKE

Round trip 9.6 km (6 mi) or less
Allow 3 hours
Old logging roads
Good June to October

The amount of travel on foot you do on this trip is proportionate to the delight you get from walking in forest and the degree of concern you have for your vehicle. You may park just off Highway 101 and give yourself a round trip of 9.6 km (6 mi); alternatively, you may drive to a little beyond a power line right-of-way or, if you care to, drive a short distance along the old logging road beyond this, overgrown and puddly though it is.

To reach whichever of these starting points you choose, drive northwest on Highway 101 from the traffic light in Sechelt for 11 km (6.8 mi) to where a road cuts back sharp right. Turn off here and the power line is a short distance in; cross its right-of-way and continue heading south, ignoring a road that joins yours at right angles from the left. For a short time you have the power line on your right just visible through trees, but, as you stay left at the next two forks, you gradually swing away from it and into dense second-growth forest that looks about ripe for thinning.

As you progress, you see one or two minor roads going off to the left or right, but you stay with the main track, eventually crossing, on a wooden bridge that has seen better days, a small creek flowing from left to right. Now you rise for a short distance and cross the same creek, though, of course, it is now flowing from right to left. Soon thereafter, glinting through trees, you see water: your lake. You are not quite at your destination yet, however. Continue north a little way and go right at the next fork. This track brings you to a small open area used for picnics and camping on the north shore of the lake.

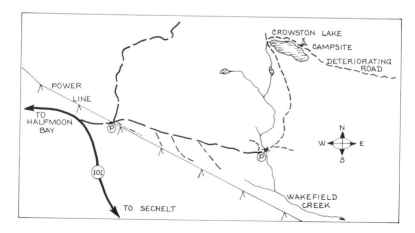

Campsite by Crowston Lake

Apart from this one spot, Crowston Lake is completely embowered in forest, and it looks utterly remote from the haunts of men. In its waters, lending colour to the scene, are beds of water lilies and, of course, there are waterfowl to test your knowledge of ornithology.

One note: The trail may be wet so good boots are necessary.

Heading seaward from Smuggler Cove

SECHELT

106 SMUGGLER COVE

Round trip 5 km (3.1 mi)
Allow 1.5 hours
Trail and track
Good much of the year

Though this is classed as a marine park by B.C.'s Park and Outdoor Recreation Division, landlubbers can sample its beauties by making use of a foot trail beginning at a parking area on Brooks Road 5 km (3 mi) west of Highway 101, which you leave 14.8 km (9 mi) beyond the traffic signal in Sechelt (watch for park access signs).

Having reached the parking spot, set off on the designated foot trail, noting at its beginning a nurse log with three good-sized trees growing from it angled over to make an arch across your path. Next, on your right, comes a one-time lake bed, then impressive forest, followed by an interesting looking marshy tract on your left. All in all, your route does not lack variety. Finally you emerge at the head of the cove where the official trail ends at present; a path, however, continues westwards along the south shore of the cove, splitting a short distance in.

If you follow the right fork, you rise a little above the bay and, in so doing, get some sense of the intricately indented shoreline. This track eventually peters out on an open headland facing south, but you may, if you wish, explore westwards to the main point. You will not be disappointed. As well as views of various islands, you have the rocky coastline, its rocks strewn with shells dropped by seabirds in order to get at their contents, an operation conducted with much raucous calling. Nor is the vegetation without interest, consisting as it does of a mixture of arbutus and salal. Had you taken the left fork back at the cove, you would work south across the narrow peninsula to a little secret cove, utterly remote and peaceful, a perfect spot for rest and contemplation.

There is the possibility of more official trails being created in this park, giving access to the cove's north side. The existing ones, however, make for perfectly satisfying walking in an area of supreme natural beauty.

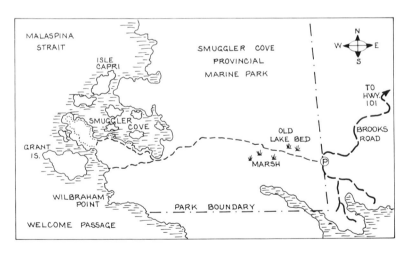

Admiring the view from Mount Daniel

SECHELT

107 MOUNT DANIEL

Round trip 5.6 km (3.5 mi)
Allow 2.5 hours
High point 420 m (1375 ft)
Elevation gain 327 m (1075 ft)
Marked route
Good June to October

This miniature mountain, once supposed to have been associated with initiation rites of the Sechelt Indians, provides an interesting adventure outing, with a superb view over Pender Harbour, its islets, bays, and peninsulas to round off the experience. Mount Daniel is the double summit seen on your left front as you drive north on Highway 101 towards Garden Bay Road junction, 5.8 km (3.6 mi) beyond the Madeira Park fork.

Go left as for Garden Bay and drive 3.2 km (2 mi) to the high point where an old road goes off left. Park here. As you set off on foot along the track, you realize that its most recent use was an access to a garbage dump, and however picturesque castoffs become after a decent period, there is nothing aesthetic about recently abandoned fridges, bedsprings, and other relics. Stay left twice, changing direction the second time and reaching a point where the road is blocked by old treeroots and the like. On the left side of this obstruction the trail, marked with tapes, takes off through a thicket of alder.

Keep a careful eye on the tapes as you gradually work round to the right, with luxurious growth of ferns on either side of your route. Steadily you rise; the fern changes to salal, and higher still you may have to negotiate a few deadfalls. After an hour's walking, you reach a bluff where the last vestiges of the one-time logging road end; a taped trail, however, continues south and this brings you to the main summit in another ten minutes or so. But— there is little view.

For this, you must look right for tapes that lead you to an open rock where the above lack is amply remedied; Garden Bay is right at your feet and Beaver Island stretches to the southwest. Here is a spot for contemplation, especially on a warm summer evening, with the westering sun etching the Vancouver Island mountains across the strait. It is a natural temple that you will be loath to leave.

On your way down, you may notice a few tapes off to your right. These would be on your left while you were ascending, but they are not very visible and you miss little if you ignore them. They do lead to the north summit but it lacks the fine views of its neighbour, so only if you are an indefatigable walker will you take this side trip to look through trees towards Sakinaw Lake.

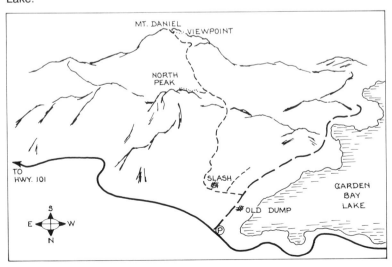

108 SKOOKUMCHUCK NARROWS

Round trip 8 km (5 mi)
Allow 3 hours
Forest trail
Good all year

Anyone who visits the Sechelt Peninsula and fails to pay respects to this natural wonder is missing an unforgettable experience; and it is free in return for expenditure of the small amount of energy required to walk on good, virtually level trails. The shoreline by the great tidal race is provincial parkland, too, so that you are free of attempts at exploition of a scene of great beauty.

To reach the beginning of the trail, turn right off Highway 101 at the Egmont signpost, a little short of the Powell River ferry terminal at Earls Cove. Drive 5.4 km (3.4 mi) on this roller coaster of a road, passing two lakes, North and Waugh, before coming to the parking lot just short of a country store. Follow the trail down a small creek, which it eventually crosses on a footbridge before climbing uphill behind some cabins whose waterlines share the right-of-way. Soon, however, signs of human settlement disappear and you are alone with the forest, a healthy second-growth, its floor carpeted with salal, red-flowering currant, and a variety of ferns.

After about a mile you see water through the trees, but as you come closer, you recognize it for the surface of another lake, not the inlet you are seeking. Still among trees, the trail follows its southern shoreline, then leaves it behind. Next, some 2.8 km (1.7 mi) from the start of your walk, you come to the first dividing of the ways; the left-hand trail leads to boat moorings, toilets, and North Point, and its right-hand fork is anonymous as it goes off a little uphill. Nevertheless, following it may be the more rewarding choice.

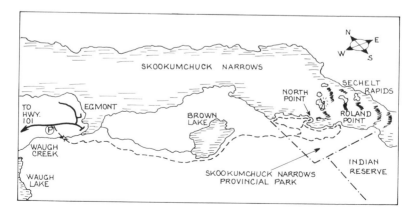

Tide race at North Point

If you do so, you eventually come to a notice announcing the proximity of the Narrows, and soon you emerge on a brow of rock overlooking the great race. Then, as you follow the coast trail back, you have varied opportunities to watch the tide flowing into or out of Sechelt Inlet, noting its great whirlpools and eddies as well as the tremendous rush of white water. Two points, Rowland and North, give grandstand views of the spectacle from the inlet to its mountain background, but the great attraction is the unresisting flow of water over the submarine rock ledges.

On resuming your journey from North Point, continue along the rocky bluffs on the edge of the forest to the boat moorings, in a sheltered cove where the still water contrasts with the violence of the inlet. From here to the trail junction is only a matter of minutes and thence you simply retrace your steps.

Finally, a word on names. It would be inspiring if the person who named Egmont did so with the chords of Beethoven's great overture ringing in his ears as an aural counterpart to the visible grandeur of the scene. In contrast, Skookumchuck is the Chinook term for "powerful water," though it is interesting that "skookum" in Salishan originally meant "demon," a not unlikely connotation.

109 AMBROSE LAKE

Round trip 4.8 km (3 mi)
Allow 1.5 hours
Old logging road
Good June to October

Not only is this ecological reserve attractive in itself, the trail to it also provides a fine view over Agamemnon Channel to Nelson Island, two names associated with Britain's one-time naval greatness. To enjoy this trip with the bonus just mentioned, continue on Highway 101 past Egmont Road for 800 m, then, just after Jervis Inlet Road and before the warning lights for the Earls Cove ferry, turn sharp left but, after a few metres, go right on Timberline Road. Follow this road to its end just past Cedar Ridge Place and before the B.C. Hydro power line that runs at right angles to it. Park.

From here, go right and stay more or less parallel with the power line, ignoring a right fork a few minutes after you set off. The track, an old logging road, rises gradually till you come to the place where the wires abruptly change direction and swoop north over the channel to Nelson Island. At this point, step a few paces right across the salal and you find yourself on a clear bluff that drops steeply to the water below, an inspiring viewpoint. Continuing southwards, stay right at the next fork then begin descending a little till you see water glinting through the trees. Here is your objective.

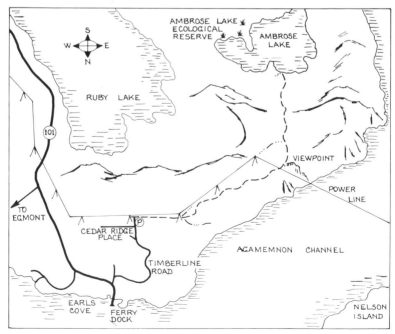

View over Agamemnon Channel to Nelson Island.

At the lakeshore you see a small bluff to the left. Scramble up this bluff with its soft carpet of moss to better appreciate the beauty of the scene, and its utter peace, the silence broken by only the occasional duck call or the lonely cry of the loon. Humble forms of life are present, too, in the marsh at the lake's edge: tadpoles, frogs, and other manifestations of bog ecology. It is to be hoped that the lake will long retain its reserve status for the delight of venturesome walkers who appreciate the peace of natural surroundings.

ADDITIONAL WALKS

The outings listed here, with a brief note on their respective approaches, are either short (of at most an hour's duration), need no further description, or their trails are still in process of development.

1. GREATER VANCOUVER

Annacis Island: From S.E. Marine Drive on the western boundary of New Westminster, cross Queensborough Bridge onto Lulu Island and go over the second bridge to Annacis. The walk is at the island's east end.

Belcarra Park: Drive through Port Moody and turn left on Ioco Road (see Walk 52). Go right on and remain with Belcarra Road to its end on Burrard Inlet. Trail runs east from the park.

Iona Island Park: Turn off Oak Street Bridge on Sea Island Way, cross Sea Island Bridge, go right on Airport Road, left on Grauer, right again on McDonald, and left on Ferguson.

John Hendry Park: Turn south on Victoria Drive from the 1900 block of East 12th Avenue in Vancouver and go one more block to the east on 15th.

Minnekhada Park: This regional park, north of Port Coquitlam, is only now being developed. To reach it, follow the approach directions for Walk 56, its entrance being about 4 km (2.5 mi) beyond the turn onto Victoria Drive. For current information, check with GVRD Parks by calling (604) 731-1155.

Queen Elizabeth Park: Go east from Cambie Street on West 30th for this, the highest point in Vancouver city.

Queen's Park: From 12th Street in New Westminster turn east on 6th Avenue for parking.

Renfrew Ravine: This neat little park is located east of Renfrew Street between East 19th and East 22nd in Vancouver.

Ron McLean Park: This pretty ravine park in Burnaby is reached from Gilley Street, which links Kingsway and S.E. Marine Drive. From Gilley, turn east on Portland Street to reach its entrance.

Van Dusen Botanical Gardens: Parking for this botanical display is located on the west side of Oak Street at West 37th Avenue in the city (admission charge).

2. FRASER DELTA

Bota Gardens: Open between April and October, these gardens are reached by turning west off Highway 99 on Steveston Highway, then going north on No. 5 Road (admission charge).

Burns Bog: Turn west off Scott Road (120th Street) in North Delta. Go west on 80th Avenue to 108th Street. Turn left again and look for the Nature Reserve sign at the Monroe Drive intersection.

Gravesend Reach: From Highway 99, just north of Massey Tunnel, go east on Steveston Highway. Turn right on a road (signposted "Garbage Dump"!) that turns south to the river.

Ladner Harbour Park: Turn off Highway 99 at the Ladner exit just south of the Massey Tunnel. Follow River Road west, then turn north at the bridge across a slough.

Peace Arch Park: On the Canada–U.S. border off Highway 99 a little north of Blaine.

Semiahmoo Trail: This historic trail has its northern terminus (with marker sign) south of the Nikomekl River at Crescent Road just west of King George Highway's turnoff from 99. From here, proceed east along Crescent Road to find the trail close to the one-roomed Elgin School.

Steveston Island: Approachable only by boat or by a causeway at low tide (underwater at other times). For road access, turn south on No. 2 Road from Steveston Highway on Lulu Island and go left on Dyke Road to parking by the causeway. A little east, the restored London Farm Heritage Site is also of interest.

Tsawwassen Beach: From south of Massey Tunnel, turn off Highway 99 on to Highway 17 and follow this to the landward end of the ferry terminal. Park on the south side of the road and walk south towards Point Roberts.

3. FRASER RIVER NORTH

Burnt Hill (Pine Mountain): At present the trail begins on the east side of Rannie Road (see Walk 59) 2.7 km (1.7 mi) north of Sturgeon Slough in a narrow belt of woodland. The Fish and Wildlife Branch has plans for a nature information centre in this area.

Cascade Creek Falls. (See Walk 65) On Sylvester Road drive 1 km (0.6 mi) north of the Cascade Creek picnic site, turn right on Ridge View Road, and continue about 800 m to park just below a gate. Walk uphill to a switchback bend where a rough trail descends to the right.

Cliff Park: From Dewdney Trunk Road about 5.6 km (3.5 mi) east of Haney turn south on 252nd Street for this picturesque stretch of Kanaka Creek.

Hayward Lake: Go north from Lougheed Highway at Ruskin for 3.2 km (2 mi) to Ruskin Dam. Short trails follow the shoreline from each end of the dam.

Kilby Historic Park: Just east of Highway 7's crossing of the Harrison River, turn south at the marker.

Neilson Regional Park: Between Mission City and Hatzic, turn north on Dewdney Trunk Road from Lougheed Highway. Carry straight on at Draper Street where the trunk road goes off west. From Draper, turn right on McEwen Avenue and follow park signs after you swing left on East Edwards Street. The park is by Hatzic Lake.

Rolley Lake Park: Turn north off Dewdney Trunk Road 1.6 km (1 mi) west of Stave Falls. The park is 3.2 km (2 mi) from the highway.

Stave Lake: From just east of the dam at Stave Falls on Dewdney Trunk Road, a trail goes north along the shore for a short distance.

Westminster Abbey: At the eastern end of Mission City turn north off Lougheed Highway on Stave Lake Street. Go right on Dewdney Trunk Road at the T-junction, then after some 500 m, go right again.

4. HARRISON LAKE WEST

Chehalis River: Turn north off Lougheed Highway on Harrison Lake West Road at Harrison Mills. The trail goes upstream from the Forest Service campground on the north side of the bridge.

Francis Lake: Drive north just over 19 km (12 mi) from Harrison Mills to the turnoff left for the Forest Service campsite. The trail runs round the lake.

Sunrise Lake: The route to this wilderness recreation site (Forest Service) goes off to the west of the lake road nearly 38 km (almost 24 mi) from Harrison Mills just south of the approach to Harrison Lookout (see Walk 68).

Weaver Creek: The salmon spawning grounds are 11.2 km (7 mi) north of Harrison Mills near the end of blacktop. Spawning season is normally in mid-October.

5. FRASER RIVER SOUTH

Bridal Veil Falls: Turn south off Highway 1 at Popkum, about 1.6 km (1 mi) east of the Agassiz-Rosedale junction.

Chilliwack Mountain Viewpoint: From Highway 1 east of its crossing of Vedder Canal, go north on Lickman Road till that turns right. Go left uphill to the trail on the left of an old building.

Hunter Creek Falls: Hunter Creek rest area is to the right of Highway 1 as you go east 25.5 km (16 mi) beyond the Agassiz-Rosedale turnoff. Park close to the creek and head upstream.

McGillivray Game Preserve: Turn north off Highway 1 at Lickman Interchange west of Chilliwack. Turn left on Cannor Frontage Road and follow it west, crossing the C.N. Railway en route. The preserve lies beyond the lumberyard and close to the Fraser.

Minter Gardens: Turn north of Highway 1 on Highway 9 (Agassiz-Rosedale). Go left for the entrance (admission charge).

Thacker Mountain: At Hope, turn off Highway 3 along 6th Avenue (Hope Golf Course sign). Go right on Kawkawa Lake Road then left after crossing the Coquihalla River. Turn left again towards a new development, then right uphill.

Vancouver Game Farm: Having gone south off Highway 1 on 264th Street (Highway 13), drive a short distance to the entrance (admission charge).

6. FRASER CANYON

Boothroyd Microwave Station: Turn east off the Trans-Canada Highway 10.6 km (6.6 mi) north of Boston Bar. The approach goes left after 800 m, passing some new homesteads.

Old Alexandra Bridge: Some 250 m north of the present bridge a picnic site on the west side of the road provides parking. From here follow the old canyon road down to the river crossing.

7. HIGHWAY 99 (Squamish-Whistler)

Alexander Falls: From the highway, 4 km (2.5 mi) north of Brandywine Falls Park, turn west and drive 8 km (5 mi) on a dirt road to a Forest Service recreation site.

Alta Lake Picnic Site: This is located west of the road a short distance north of Whistler Mountain gondola terminal.

Britannia Mine Museum: The parking lot is just east of the highway in Britannia Beach village (admission charge).

Murrin Park: At the top of the long hill between Britannia Beach and Squamish. Parking is on the west side of the road.

Porteau Marine Park: This provincial recreation area is located just west of the highway 12.8 km (8 mi) north of Lions Bay.

Shannon Falls: These are a little east of the road a short distance south of Squamish. The park also contains nature walks and a logging museum.

8. SECHELT

Chaster Park (Gower Point): At School Road the main street of Gibsons becomes Gower Point Road. Follow this road south along the coast to the park.

Gray Creek Falls: From the traffic light in Sechelt village, turn right and drive north on Inlet Road for 8.4 km (5.2 mi). The trail goes upstream on the creek's south bank from just before the bridge.

Homesite Creek and Caves: Turn right off Highway 101 at a point 2.1 km (1.3 mi) north of Brooks Road, itself north of Halfmoon Bay. Drive 1.5 km (1 mi) and park at a fork near the trailhead.

Klein Lake: Fork east from the highway on Egmont Road a little south of Earls Cove. Drive 1.6 km (1 mi) along this road, then turn right for another 3 km (1.9 mi).

Pender Hill: Drive west on Garden Bay Road from Highway 101 just south of Pender Harbour Secondary School. Fork right on Irvine's Landing Road to just before its junction with Lee Road. The trail rises steeply from right side of road.

INDEX